# ENDING THE WAR WITH MYSELF

*Loving Myself As God Does*

**Anna "Micky" Land MS, LPC**

*Ending the War with Myself:*
*Loving Myself As God Does*

ISBN 978-0-9761668-3-2

Published by Stratagem Press
PO Box 1697
Woodstock, GA 30188

www.endingthewarwithmyself.com

Printed in the United States of America

Editor: Julie Anne Cross, PhD
Production & Print Management: Robert Campbell
Cover Design: Julie Anne Cross, PhD

# TABLE OF CONTENTS

# DEDICATION

I dedicate this book to John Britton Land who is present with the Lord; to my husband Roger; and to the next two generations: my son and daughter-in-law, Kelly and Kara Land, along with my two grandchildren, Walker and Sarah Land. God's favor is on each of them.

And

To all my clients who honored me by pouring out their hearts. To Dr. Marlene Huyler who challenged me to do this and encouraged me all along the way. To Beth Geary, Shirley Goodwin, Charles Brooks, Elaine Baker and Amy Howard who were my cheerleaders. To Ashley Wille, who wrote the creative prose at the beginning of each chapter with such inspiration; to Carol Scott, my spiritual mother, mentor, and long time friend; to Sally Hayes who helped with the proofing; and to Dr. James Saxon, associate pastor extraordinaire at my church, who helped with theological issues.

# *GRACE IS*

*Grace is victorious in my life when I come*
*To the place where I can accept myself*
*For who I am and where I am regardless*
*Of my past or present failures.*

*Grace is victorious in my life when I can*
*Say about myself what God says about me:*
*I am forgiven.*
*I am loved by God.*
*I am a child of God.*
*I am righteous in God's sight.*
*I am accepted in the beloved.*

*Grace is victorious in my life when I know*
*And experience God as my best friend*
*With my best interests at heart.*

*Grace is victorious in my life when I know*
*And experience I am at one with God,*
*And at one with myself.*

*Grace is victorious in my life when*
*I can rest in the Sabbath rest of God,*
*And befriend and encourage myself as God does;*
*Knowing and experiencing His mercy, His grace,*
*His forgiveness and His guidance; because I*
*Treat myself with God's mercy, grace, forgiveness,*
*And Godly guidance.*

By Anna "Micky" Land

# OVERVIEW AND HOW TO USE THIS BOOK

*Ending the War with Myself* represents one person's journey. I am not a theologian. I am a Christian who happens to be a licensed professional counselor (LPC). As such, I have had many opportunities to interact with people, hear their hearts, their pain and realities; and then share with them the truths found in this book. These truths are important to me because I have experienced them myself.

I believe I have some insights for Christians that are often not clearly explained in our churches. These insights will not be anything new, because they are based on scripture and my growing relationship with God. They may well give you a new way of thinking about yourself and God.

This book targets the emotions, wounding and thoughts of the Christian. From the day we are born, our emotions are impacted both positively and negatively by external and internal experiences. You will probably find that your internal experience is often very similar to what I have experienced internally over my lifetime. The external circumstances of our lives may be profoundly different and your circumstances may or may not have been 100 times more filled with wounding than mine. What will be the same, however, is how our external circumstances have impacted and wounded our souls.

If the wounds we have experienced are not dealt with, they will continue to haunt our present relationships. Our unhealed wounds can infect our relationships with those closest to us. More importantly, our wounds adversely impact our relationship with God. God doesn't see us differently, and He continues to love us at all times; but from our perspective, we may feel the pain from our wounds instead of feeling His love. We puzzle about why we are not experiencing God's freedom, grace, and joy promised to us in the New Testament.

If you have not been in counseling or a group targeting recovery, this book may lead you into an unfamiliar world. *Recovery* in a Christian context means *recovering from the effects of the fall of man*. Many of the concepts may be new to you. This is an inner journey that will allow God to touch and heal your heart of hearts. As Christians we learn that our minds are to be renewed. Why is this so? There are harmful ways of thinking, being, feeling and acting that need healing. Bible studies and sermons aid this process, as do Christian counseling and groups. Christian counseling, unlike most Bible studies, is a bit like alternative medicine. We do not only deal with the outward, or surface, behavior in counseling. We look for the root cause and seek to work with God's Spirit to remove or heal the root that impacts behavior.

I have several goals for you as you read this book. The first is a desire for you to like yourself as a unique creation, a special child of God. As I have worked with my clients, I consistently see a universal plight: most people seem to have a strong dislike of themselves. When we genuinely dislike ourselves, you will see how we unknowingly block ourselves from receiving what is already available for us from God. When we can't receive what God has promised to us, we live in emotional turmoil and limit our potential for use in the kingdom of God.

The second goal is to help you live in the emotional and spiritual freedom and peace Christ died to give you. Because we were born into a sinful, fallen world, we all experienced wounds as children that may continue to impact our current relationships. When we are wounded, we believe a lie told to us by the one who wounds us, or we interpret the event in a way that we tell ourselves a lie. These are lies about who we are, and they sneak into our belief system. We must uncover these lies, or they can block our experience of the grace of God in many areas of our lives. The enemy of our souls works to use these lies to block our understanding of the love of God from our hearts. As long as we are unaware of what is available to us from God and of what is blocking our progress in the Christian faith, the effects of the wounds, sins, and dislike of self will hinder our living life to its fullest in relational and spiritual matters. When we experience God's grace to heal our hearts, He replaces poisonous, toxic lies with His truths to heal the effects of the wounds.

Thirdly, I desire to get the word out to Christians and non-Christians that God is not who the world thinks He is. He is too often represented only as the God of wrath and punishment. God must judge sin, because He is holy. Because God is full of grace, He sent Jesus who has already taken God's wrath and punishment for the believer's sin. When we accept God's grace through faith in what Jesus did for us, there is no condemnation left for the believer! As Christians we are now free to experience God's love. Too often, we believe God is still judging every imperfection, so we become hyper-vigilant about measuring up…and so begins *the war with myself.* I pray from these pages a new reality of God will emerge and you will end the war with yourself in your heart of hearts.

The fourth goal for you is to live a more realistic, balanced and authentic Christian life. Christians are generally fearful of being authentic. As a model of authenticity I choose to use my own life experiences for most of the examples. Carl Rogers, a psychiatrist who developed client-centered therapy stressed, "What is most personal and unique in each of us is probably the very element which would, if it were shared or expressed, speak most deeply to others." Although Rogers did not claim to be a Christian, I believe he hit on a truth that when we share from our heart of hearts, it speaks deeply to the one listening. Being authentic is true ministry, giving hope and grace to others. I hope as I share my frustrations, struggles, insights, and victories, I will speak deeply to you.

Some might say I have not addressed the justice and wrath of God, only the love of God. I purposely do so. I minister to people who already know they are sinners. They are broken and have come for help. They are stuck at some point in their lives and want to move forward with God. All serious Christians seem to understand they do not measure up to God's standards. In my fifteen years of practice I've only experienced two arrogant clients who needed to hear of God's justice. One claimed to be a Christian and the other did not. Each came once. I leave the arrogant ones for someone else's ministry: I have been called to the wounded.

You will find that many of the chapters overlap in content. Anytime you examine God's principles for life in Christ, we find that like a diamond there are many facets: facets that make a whole. The content may overlap as each facet is related to the others, and as you grow to see how they fit together. I hope these chapters are filled with God's principles that will help you experience more of the whole of Christ.

The prose at the beginning of each chapter was written by my friend Ashley Wille. She and I met a number of years ago and developed a relationship based on our common experience of the goodness and grace of God. We served on the board of a ministry when the idea of a book was suggested and seemed plausible. She and others encouraged me to write this book. Previously I read some of Ashley's work and was impressed with her creativity and the way she expressed her thoughts in words. In her prose she paints a vivid picture for the reader. I think you will like what she has composed for each chapter.

In these chapters, I will walk with you to help you uncover your wounds and discover what lies may have blocked God's grace in your own life. Each section ends with a question designed to help you apply truth to your heart and to discover who you really are as a child of God. Many books talk about self esteem, how to make it stronger, and how to use it to get what you want. I have coined the term *God Esteem* to challenge our idea of self esteem. God Esteem is similar to, but radically different from self esteem. Rather than trying to dress up our selves to look good, I propose that we accept ourselves as we are by removing our own judgment and condemnation. We can begin to see ourselves as God sees us, creating a godly sense of wellbeing in Christ. This is God Esteem. I am frequently surprised by how many committed, Jesus-loving, Bible-teaching Christians do not know the principles I will be sharing with you.

This book is not for those who can't imagine why others have problems. Your life is fine. Thank you. And if it was not, who in their right mind would admit it, much less delve into it? If you are OK with impression management, managing your moves to look competent and in control, proving you can indeed be the master of your own soul; then this book is not for you. If, however, you are sick and tired of being sick and tired of having to be strong and holding everything together; or if you feel weak, inadequate, and without hope of anything ever changing, then this book is for you.

I pray God will use this book to drop any head knowledge of God into your heart so that you may experience the love of God. "Experience far surpasses head knowledge" (from

Ephesians 13:14- 21, Amplified version). God's goal is to heal our souls so we might actualize what He has already done (past tense) in our spirits. Ultimately, the Holy Spirit intends to lead us into God's Sabbath rest.

I have purposely used the Amplified version of the bible for all citations. I personally enjoy this version because the Amplified Bible paraphrase offers a fuller understanding of the original Greek and gives us greater insight to the meaning of the scriptures.

*Take these thoughts with you as you delve into each chapter and discover how:*

1. **Your relationship with yourself impacts you, others, and the kingdom of God.**
2. **Your wounds and toxic lies adversely impact your relationship with yourself, others, and God.**
3. **God is more merciful than you ever imagined.**
4. **Authenticity is what the world wants to see in Christians.**
5. **Seeing yourself through God's eyes will revolutionize the quality of your life and ministry.**

In Christ,
*Anna Catherine Oberry*
*Land, "Micky"*

# HOW TO USE THIS BOOK

### *Taking an Inner Journey with the Lord*

This book is designed to help you engage in an inner journey with the Lord. The questions are optional, but taking time to answer the questions will give you personal insights that you probably won't get if you just read. Taking an inner journey means getting in touch with your innermost thoughts and feelings, and sharing them with the Lord, so He can share His thoughts for you in them. This takes effort, and time to think through your thoughts and feelings. Some of you may not be naturally intuitive, and this may feel unfamiliar and even uncomfortable for you. Journaling your thoughts will help you take this inner journey. Most sections in the book end with a question or two for you to journal your answers. Buy a spiral bound notebook and use it to journal your answers to the questions. The questions are numbered in each chapter, so that you can number your answers as you go. This book can be done individually or with a group, but your journal is yours alone, to share or not to share.

Answer the questions with your honest thoughts and feelings, not just with what you consider to be the correct Biblical answer. Giving the correct Biblical answer is what most people do in Bible studies and only address the facts. This Journey with God is about addressing your heart. God wants you to be gut wrenching honest with your answers. Once you and He are in agreement about any part of your life that misses His perfect will, it is then and only then that He can heal you.

Prior to reading the questions pray, asking the Holy Spirit to reveal to you what He wants you know about yourself. Don't filter your initial thoughts. Being honest with yourself and God is necessary for change and healing. Write what immediately comes to your mind. Don't worry about what anyone else might think, because the journal is just for you. Everyone's answers will be different, because our lives are different. Don't condemn yourself, because God is not condemning you for what you may discover. He knows our confusion before we do! Take your heart to the Lord to heal. Whatever you discover, confess anything you need to confess, then quietly listen to what God has to say to you regarding His love for you. Journal what you hear from the Lord. May God bless you — reach down and touch your heart — as you come to Him for healing and growth.

*Books can be ordered at* http://www.EndingtheWarwith Myself.com.

# CHAPTER 1

# SOMETHING IS WRONG!

## Why Don't I Connect with God's Love?

### The False Self

I live inside my cloak. It is who I am. Or at least who I think I am. I actually pieced it together myself over the years. It is made up of convenient ideas and labels I use to protect, defend, justify, validate, and promote myself. Do you see my eyes peeking out? My cloak is so well woven you can't tell where it ends and I begin. Inside my cloak I am all about me. I will tell you things about myself to impress you and make you like me and think I'm great.

Recently, I heard an unsettling truth that this cloak of mine is actually not who I am. This is most confusing to me because this identity is all I have ever known. Deep inside my cloak I am a wounded child. My cloak is a shield of protection for me. But the problem is my shield is made up of lies, and it keeps me locked inside and everyone else locked out. I want to think that the cloak is my friend, but it is not

*my friend. And since I am a child of God, if I intend
to grow, I must come to face the truth that this cloak
of mine is not who I am. Where do I go from here?*

*By Ashley Wille*

We need to experience love and acceptance as much as we need air and water. This longing to be loved is played out in every facet of our lives. We are driven to do and to be and to act in ways we hope will make us desirable and acceptable to the significant people in our lives: a boss, a husband, a girlfriend, a family member and even God. Even though I intellectually knew God loved me, I did not experience God's love in my heart. I discovered the key to experiencing God's love is accepting God's grace in all areas of my life. Accepting God's grace opens the door to experiencing God's love. I will share my journey of accepting God's grace and running into the arms of God's love. I pray that you too will experience this journey.

## Reasons We Don't Connect with the Love of God

When I was twelve years old I inadvertently began a war with myself. At fourteen I began a war with God. By the time I was 30 the war with God ended as I accepted His Son as my Lord and Savior. And yet, the war with myself continued for years. I didn't realize how this war blocked the peace, joy, love, and grace promised to me in the New Testament.

Something was wrong. As I share with you several reasons why we don't connect with the love of God, take a few moments to consider and write down your thoughts about the questions relating to each section. Hopefully this will help you understand and evaluate how each reason may or may not be impacting you. I differentiate between head knowledge and heart knowledge. This book is about personally experiencing the love of God.

## We Dislike Ourselves

We may learn about the love and the grace of God, but when it comes to our private thought lives we often condemn, criticize, and judge ourselves harshly. In short we just don't like ourselves. Disliking ourselves is the number one, overriding reason we don't experience God's grace and love in our hearts. If we were only healed of this one error we could experience God's love and grace. The split between us and God began in the Garden of Eden with Adam and Eve's disobedience. Their sin resulted in a relational separation from God, from their fellow man, and from their true selves. This split still happens to us today.

I experienced this separation when I was twelve years old. Before this, life was a joy for me; I felt connected to my true self and I enjoyed being *me*. But in seventh grade, I had a mean-spirited teacher who berated and put me down on and off for the entire year. By the end of the seventh grade, I came to see myself through my teacher's eyes. Surprisingly, after that I took up where she left off, berating, chastising, and judging myself as unfit and stupid. The war with myself began. I had internalized her voice, spouting words like poison about how worthless I was. These poisonous, toxic lies took over and I turned against myself. Because I did not understand what had happened, I spent years putting myself down. Negative self-talk impacted every aspect of my life and even began to mold my future. Relationships became difficult. I saw myself as less than others and not important enough to have relationships with certain people I admired. I second guessed my every decision. I expected and then accepted defeat.

As a counselor, I observe this *war with myself* phenomena in 90% of my clients. Being wounded by someone not expected to be an enemy, the person abandons their true self and blindly joins with this enemy, railing themselves. This begins their own *war with myself*. This war significantly contributes to depression, anxiety, relational schisms, and spiritual defeat. If we could hear the thought life of many who believe in God's grace, I think we would be shocked to hear how abusive we are to ourselves. In disparaging words, we put down, criticize, justify, deny, drive, lie, and deceive ourselves. We find ourselves living in a self-constructed expectation of perfection or a self-constructed acceptance of defeat rather than resting in God's real grace and will for our lives.

One example from my own life illustrates how I took a small oversight and made it into a huge condemnation in my thoughts. I was seeing clients in my counseling internship. The room I used for counseling was in the far back of the building, but as an intern I was required to leave my notes for each client in filing cabinets in the front office before leaving each day. Each evening, the advisor locked the filing cabinets for safekeeping. At the end of one day, I put on my coat and walked the long hall to the front office. My supervisor reminded me that I still needed to turn in my files. Walking back to my room, thoughts began to fly. "You are so stupid! You are one of the oldest participants in this program and you can't even remember to take the files to the front office. All the other students brought theirs up front, and they heard her tell you to get yours. Now they all know how incompetent you really are! Are you sure you can pull off this graduate school thing?" I was filled with shame. I was the one producing the shame caused by my berating self-talk for such a minuscule oversight. Perfectionism won and I was defeated. I didn't sleep well that night.

## 1. Are you at war with yourself? How would you describe this war with yourself?

### *We Nullify God's Grace*

It may never have occurred to you that a negative relationship with yourself could keep you from experiencing God's grace and God's love. Paul declares in Galatians 2:22, "I do not set aside and invalidate and frustrate and nullify the grace [unmerited favor] of God." We can understand from Paul's comment that if Paul does not nullify or frustrate the grace of God, then there is the potential for each of us to do just that.

God's grace is there and God's love is there, always available. We judge and condemn ourselves, rather than accepting His grace and receiving His love as we walk with the Lord. God declares triumphantly we are His children, accepted in the beloved, loved, forgiven, joint heirs with Jesus Christ, and free from condemnation. We fight God and say, "No God I'm not special. I don't even like myself." With this response, we are choosing to oppose God and refuse to walk in agreement with Him. When we call ourselves unclean while God calls us clean (John 13:10), might we be sinning against ourselves as well as sinning against God? When we sin against ourselves we further abuse and wound ourselves at our expense. The truth is we often do to ourselves what God admonishes us not to do others: we judge and condemn.

This sin against ourselves becomes a negative witness for Christ as we do not exhibit what it means to be redeemed by grace through faith. We may think we are concealing how we honestly feel. We really believe we have let God down and we feel unacceptable to Him. Believing the lie that we are unacceptable to God keeps us in bondage. We think we know God loves us and at the same time we tell ourselves how unlovable we are. This contradiction creates internal conflict for us. Amos 3:3 says, "How then can two men walk together except they be in agreement?" God defines truth and we negate that truth by believing something contrary to His revealed will. We nullify our experience of the love of God by rejecting the grace of God and trying to be good enough on our own.

**2. In what ways might you be nullifying the grace of God? Journal your thoughts and feelings about this.**

### We Hide from God and Others

The second reason we do not accept God's grace to connect with the love of God: we protect and hide ourselves because we are deeply aware of our imperfections. If we would stop and listen to our hearts, we would find an underlying fear of exposing our shortcomings. Fear of self-exposure can drive us to hide what we perceive to be undesirable thoughts, facts and behaviors. Denying and hiding our imperfections is irrational for the Christian. God gave us His grace, forgiveness and love so we would be free, honest, authentic and confessional to God, and to other Christians. God cries out to each of us, "Come child, I can help you. Come child, I don't judge you any more. Come child, I can give you rest."

T. John Powell told a friend he was writing a book titled, *Why Am I Afraid to Tell You Who I Am?* The friend spontaneously replied, "Do you really want an answer to your question?" John said, "Yes, of course I do. What is it?" The friend responded, "If I tell you who I am, and you reject who I am, then that is all I have to give." In this man's answer we can feel him saying, "I know I do not measure up and if I were to tell you how much I don't measure up and you were to reject me, I would have nothing left to offer you; therefore, I remain silent. I must hide." So he stays in hiding. We can only be free from hiding when we stop pretending we are perfect Christians!

Keeping imperfections covered creates hypocrisy in relationships, even in our relationship with God. God knows the truth about us, but we try to hide our imperfections from God. Hypocrisy develops and shame builds within us as we try to live up to perceived Biblical and societal standards of perfection. Consciously or subconsciously we still know we are not as perfect as we work to appear. We put on masks of public behavior we think are expected from our families, friends, and churches. We hide who we are inside from others and God because we are fearful our imperfections will be exposed in the agony of our naked shame and rejection. We play the game, hiding our authentic selves, never being real with others.

For years after becoming a Christian at age thirty, I protected myself by hiding in this way. My mind knew what Jesus had done for me, but I continued to see myself as I did prior to receiving Christ. I presented to the world what I now know is called *a false-self*. Fear of what others would think of me kept me jumping through hoops when someone asked for help. I needed acceptance so I was afraid to say *no*. What would they think of me? Would they consider me selfish, not a good, obedient Christian? I began to get tired and exhausted. Then resentment set in. I became angry with myself for saying *yes*. My anger simmered and I felt used. Yet when the next person called, I would say *yes* with my mouth while my heart was screaming *no*! Fear kept me from speaking up for myself and setting healthy boundaries. I still struggle with being a people pleaser and trying to look good to others, but understanding God's grace has helped me learn to stop hiding.

### We Live in Silent Shame

We all have things about ourselves that we really don't like so well, but if we refuse to accept these imperfections we begin to live a life based in shame. We set high standards we cannot meet. We make mistakes, but we expect perfection and judge ourselves as shameful failures. Shame says, "Something is wrong with me. I am intrinsically flawed. I will never measure up. I am bad." Shame torments us, hitting us in our gut and robbing life from us. We know we really are imperfect human beings, but we are ashamed, blocking our authenticity. John Bradshaw asserts "a shamed-based person will guard against exposing his inner self to others, but more significantly, he will guard against exposing himself to himself." I would also add, exposing himself to God. Even if Christians are supposed to recognize their imperfection as being covered by God's grace, it is too painful to admit to ourselves.

Many good actions are motivated by believing *I can't let another know how lacking I am,* so we do many *right* things for the *wrong* reasons. We want to protect ourselves from ever feeling the pain of shame. The lie goes something like this: "Shame hurts so bad, I will do anything to not feel that feeling. If I am good, I will never have to feel shame again." Our motives for good behavior are often not as altruistic as we would like to imagine. On one hand we imagine God wants us to act perfectly; therefore we believe we are trying to please God. On the other hand, we are fighting to not have the gut-wrenching feelings of shame.

There is real shame and false shame. False shame is one of Satan's finest weapons. We must know how to differentiate between real shame and false shame. If you were to go out with friends, get drunk and find yourself on top of a piano in the middle of a bar singing as loud as possible, then the shame you feel tomorrow as you think about what you did would be real shame. Real shame comes from moral misconduct. False shame comes from a lie that says I should be able to measure up and be faultless.

God does not convict with shame. Shaming someone is a dysfunctional way of manipulating another person to do what you want. God does not manipulate us. God uses true conviction, not shame. Conviction is sweet. We may cry, but a burden is lifted and we feel light of heart and free. Shame keeps us trapped in a pit of fear, not admitting to ourselves or to others that we are flawed.

God knows we cannot measure up and that we are intrinsically flawed, that is why Jesus died and rose again to bring us new life. God loves and accepts us in our imperfection because Jesus paid the penalty of our sin: this is the true Gospel. A popular secular saying is "I am okay and you are okay." As a Christian we must instead remember that "I am not okay and you are not okay, and that is okay." This is Gods grace that covers our imperfection and sin as I confess it to Him.

3.  **What keeps you hiding your true self from others? Journal your thoughts and feelings about this.**

### We Try to Earn Acceptance

Sally was a real achiever, wheeling and dealing with the best of them. Smiles, praise, and even applause had rewarded her achievements since she was a child. *Perform for others and they will reward you with acceptance* became her motivation in life. This way of being and doing worked well for her in high school and in college. Sally saw herself as acceptable if she earned the acceptance of others. Soon her true feelings didn't really matter if others accepted and praised her. The more she pleased others the more opportunities came her way. She was perceived as a strong woman with a strong work ethic, so more and more responsibilities were given to her and her business grew. Others were in awe of her achievements and respected her success.

But in this American dream life, Sally was miserable. She admitted, "I got up on the stage when I was a child and started dancing and now thirty years later I have no idea how to get off the stage. My life is a nightmare marathon. I cannot let others know I am not who they think I am. They will reject and not respect me." Sally's self-talk encircled her with thoughts like, "I am a pretender, a hypocrite. Do I really love God or am I just pretending to love God? Who am I, really?" Sally had become addicted to pleasing others. She could not slow down, say no, or take time for herself. She had been dancing all these years because she believed a poisonous, toxic lie: she could earn acceptance, thinking it was the love she could not live without. The truth was that she needed God's love. She concluded, "Applause and acceptance from others has become my god."

Just as Sally tried to earn acceptance, we try to earn God's love. To earn love, we force ourselves to do whatever it takes to earn His acceptance. On some level, we know this is not the love described in the Bible, and we can't quite seem to earn it. Silent and isolated, we hide our true feelings and keep trying. Believers begin wearing what I call *Jesus masks*. "How are you today, Sister Jones?" "I am just fine! Praise the Lord!" she replies, fully aware that she and her husband are in the fight of their lives to keep their marriage together. God will accept us by His grace, but we want to be accepted by our achievements. We wear the mask.

**4. In what ways do you identify with Sally? Or do you? Journal your thoughts and feelings about this.**

### We Try to Be Strong

We often seem to have an intense conviction we must be strong and in command in all of life's circumstances. We *do life* with a stiff upper lip. Weakness is not tolerated. We may say, "Oh, I know no one is perfect." But our thought lives and actions belie our words. We know the Bible tells us how to have a relationship with Him. We need a Savior to forgive our sin, and we accept His salvation by acknowledging we have sinned, But once we accept His salvation by grace, we forget that we ever needed a savior.

At some deep level we cannot or will not admit to ourselves that Jesus came for the sick and that we fall into that category. In truth, we operate as if we need no savior. If we could become comfortable, not with sin, but with the reality we really do need a savior, then we would stop condemning ourselves, instead accepting God's grace that opens our hearts to more of God's love. We find a resting place filled with God's love once we accept in our hearts that we cannot measure up. When we fail, our attitude should be, "Thank You, Jesus, for being my Savior, because I really do need one."

5. **Do you live as if you have to be strong? Think back. Where do you think that belief came from? Journal your thoughts and feelings about this.**

### Toxic Lies Guide our Lives

Each of us was wounded in some way during our growing years; some more than others. We experience wounding in smaller or larger events at school, at home, in our neighborhood, in church, on sport teams, and in other groups. Some of the wounds we vividly remember; but some are more subtle and we may not really remember them. These events may cause us to internalize lies about ourselves that we don't even know we live by. These poisonous, toxic lies silently drive our lives.

An example of a toxic lie may be seen in how your father may have treated you as you grew up. Perhaps he had little personal interaction with you, but you noticed that when you excelled he commended you and was proud of you. You began to say to yourself, "For my father to love me, I must be successful." This statement had gradually become, "To be loved, I must be successful." We can see how toxic this false statement is when we acknowledge that we can never be always successful. *What happens when you are not successful?* You believe you will not be loved, so you strive for success at all costs. Your life is driven by this toxic lie. As a different example, you may have had a father who often slapped you, and would scream, "I wish you had never been born!" You come to believe the lie, "I am worthless and deserve to be slapped around." Your relationships with men are colored by this toxic lie, continuing to wound you with unhealthy relationships.

According to Dr. Ed Smith, "the only authority Satan has in a Christian's life is based on the lies we believe." Either an authority figure tells us a lie or we tell ourselves a lie as to who we are. We believe these lies, blocking the love of God. Until we accept the truth of God's grace about who we really are, God's love is just a concept in our minds. As God's grace shows us who we are in Christ, toxic lies are replaced with God's truth and God's love can flow into our hearts.

### We Let Pride Creep In

A client I'll call Judy shared her story, which illustrates the pride we don't recognize as it creeps in. Wiping the tears from her eyes, she explained:

*My mother was a single parent. She worked hard to put me through college. She saved me so much money by paying for undergraduate school, and then I was blessed to receive a grant to get my master's degree and my Ph.D. I was so into myself over those years I had little time for my mother. When she asked for help I would be snippy with her, sometimes just not helping her at all. She often begged me to come home to visit, saying, 'We haven't seen each other in such a very long time.' I could not get around to it. After graduation I took a job in another city. Shortly after I moved away, I received a phone call telling me my mother had suddenly passed away. I was devastated. There was so much unfinished business I had with her and now she was no longer here. I went into a depression that has lasted a number of years. I just cannot shake how mean I was to her. I have asked for forgiveness over and over again, but there is no release. I am stuck. What am I to do?*

Judy's story is similar to that of many Christians I counsel. They cannot really accept the forgiveness that their faith teaches is available to each of us, the forgiveness that Jesus died for. They know about forgiveness but do not experience God's forgiveness. When I asked Judy, "What is your self-talk like regarding these events with your mother?" She replied, "Oh, I beat myself up almost daily. I am so angry with myself," I then asked, "How does your faith play into this anger and guilt you feel?" She was puzzled. "I know God has forgiven me, but I can't seem to experience His forgiveness. "What does God's Word say about forgiveness?" I asked. "If I confess my sin, God is faithful and just to forgive my sin," she replied. (1 John 1:9) "So, has He forgiven you of your sin?" I asked. "I know He has," she said with such conviction it confused me. "Then why do you keep beating yourself up?" I asked. She replied, "Because what you say seems too easy." I questioned, "What do you mean, 'That seems too easy'?" She responded, "It just seems like I ought to have to do something to get forgiveness." "And if you do something in order to get forgiveness from God, then who will be the provider of your forgiveness?" I asked. "I guess I will," she whispered. "And if you are the provider of your forgiveness, who will get the glory?" I suggested. "I guess I will," she consented. I gently concluded, "And that will make you your own savior, not Jesus."

I explained, "It seems to me you beat yourself up because you believe you should be a strong, self-sufficient woman, but you let yourself down by not being more helpful and more compassionate with your mother. Yes, you should have been a more attentive daughter: but since you weren't, the lack of action towards your mother points out that you are not perfect. I believe the reason you really beat yourself up is because your sin exposed the fact you are inadequate. And you hate feeling inadequate, thus you hate yourself. Our pride keeps us fighting ourselves regarding our frailties and shortcomings, because we think we should get it right. You don't like feeling weak. Yet Jesus said He came for the sick, those who know they have a difficult time being all they know they should be. By refusing to accept yourself with all of your frailties, you are blocking the grace of God, the very grace you are so in need of. Instead of hating your own frailties, Judy, you might start owning them and begin to live with the truth that you are inadequate. We are all inadequate. *Stop believing the lie:* I should always be strong and competent in all areas of my life. There is only one faultless person who ever lived and His name is Jesus. Since you believe you should be faultless, whose place do you desire to take?"

"Jesus'," she responded.

I continued, "The Scriptures also tell us that you and I were born with a sin nature. That is why we need a Savior.

How do you plan to get around that truth since you desire to be faultless?" She pondered how she had been doing a pretty good job of being strong and sufficient all these years. I continued, "It is essential for Christians to accept and own that each of us is inadequate to live the life God set out in scripture. Jesus is the faultless one who lived life perfectly for us and the one who died for our sins (our inability to hit the mark of perfection); not the other way around. Owning inadequacy is not what creates your pain. It is the judging, condemning, and hating yourself for the inadequacy that creates your pain. God is not surprised you are human and that you sin. This is why He sent Jesus! You say you are a Christian, but you cannot personally receive the gift of forgiveness Jesus died to give you. In reality, pride is keeping you distanced from receiving God's gift of forgiveness. In order to receive from God the forgiveness you so desire to experience, it is necessary to admit you are one of those sin-sick, inadequate people Jesus came for." (see Matthew 9:12) "You said, 'There should be more to forgiveness than just asking God to forgive me.' Judy, why did Jesus die?" She replied, "To take all of my sins on Him and to give me forgiveness for things I do wrong." I followed, "Let me ask you one last question: Did Jesus die needlessly for you since you will not receive the forgiveness He died for?"

Ouch! She was getting the point. I asked her if she would like to pray out loud and ask God one final time to forgive her and then put down her stake on that truth, believing she is forgiven. Judy tearfully offered a beautiful, heartfelt prayer to God. She smiled to me, saying, "I feel so much lighter." The burden was lifted. I wanted the stake to hold, so I said, "Judy, when you are tempted to pick up this burden again, just tell Satan, 'I have nothing to do with that anymore. If you want to talk to someone about it, go talk to Jesus!'" We both laughed.

33

Many people have the same feelings Judy had, feeling distant from God. God's love is there, His grace is there, His acceptance is there, His forgiveness is there, His emotional healing is there, and God is there. God forgives us the moment we pray and ask for forgiveness. *Will we take the grace God is offering or will we reject God's forgiveness, proudly insisting that we must be perfect on our own?*

We can learn from observing the toxic lies driving Judy's pain. Even though she had prayed for God's forgiving grace to save her, her pride in being self-sufficient insisted that in her actions toward her mother, she should have been good, when she knew she was bad. She lived being guided by the lie that she should be able to be good on her own. Secondly, she lived by "I must be strong." If you believe you are required to be strong then when you fail, you will beat yourself up for failing. She was hiding from the reality that like the rest of us, she is inadequate to live the Christian life on her own. When we expect ourselves to be sufficient, we don't know that this means we become too proud to receive God's grace for our insufficiency. Pride creeps in and keeps us from grace, and without grace, we cannot receive God's love.

6. **What is your self-talk like? Describe it in your journal.**

### *The Effects of Childhood Wounds*

Many of the reasons we can't accept God's grace have roots in childhood wounds. As children, we learn how to treat ourselves by the ways others treat us. We may be expected to be perfect, so we expect we should be perfect, which is a toxic lie. Since we truly cannot be perfect, we soon dislike our imperfect selves. We try to be strong, but we feel false shame in that imperfection. We try to hide our real selves and earn acceptance so that the false self we show looks perfect. Under all this working and earning and trying, we are still wounded by toxic lies. If the wounds we suffered are not found, examined and healed they don't just go away with time. Wounds of our past adversely impact our inner lives and our current relationships.

Recent technology now allows us to better understand how the brain functions. Different parts of the brain perform different functions and hold different kinds of memory. Understanding how our brain holds our past pain gives us reason to go on a journey into our hearts with God so our childhood wounds can be healed.

The front of the brain, called the cerebral cortex, is the area of conscious thought, perception, and logic. The outer layer of the cerebrum is composed of gray matter and forms a cap over the rest of the brain, so the cerebral cortex has been called the *thinking cap*. It holds and organizes information and facts and works well with numbers, but it has no feelings to go with the logic. Like Mr. Spock, a Vulcan in the television and movie series, *Star Trek*, who could not feel emotion, some people have so suppressed their emotions that they operate almost exclusively out of the cerebral cortex. They operate in a superficial and informational kind of way. Cerebral individuals generally do not have deep, intimate relationships because they are too emotionally closed down to connect with others.

In the back of the brain, the limbic system holds our emotions, our pain, and our emotional experience memory. The limbic system is sometimes referred to as the *emotional brain*. It is the site of emotional states and behavior. It is the bridge between the conscious and subconscious brain. The emotional brain has no words to express itself and has no understanding of time. Any emotional pain experienced in our growing years, unless it has been dealt with and healed, is still alive in the emotional brain.

The emotional brain will override the logical thinking cap every time, unless the wound is revisited to heal the emotional memory. The emotional brain may surprise us by causing us to overreact over and over again. We may have little or no awareness we are caught in a dynamic triggered from our childhood wounds. These triggers control us and wreak havoc in our relationships. It feels like what is happening in our emotions is only our present reality. We believe the person in front of us did something to us that has been triggered in our emotional memory, so that person in front of us is to blame for our overreactions. In reality, any heightened disproportionate response is born in the emotional memory set from a past event. But we don't understand any of this, so we just judge ourselves and blame others for our bad actions. We get caught up in a self-destructive cycle. Once we are spinning reality, judging ourselves, and blaming others, it is as if we are on automatic pilot to self and relational destruction. This formidable pattern is so pervasive; I believe Satan loves to fan the fire of our self-defeating spiritual and psychological drama. Satan can easily accomplish his objective simply by letting us fly on automatic pilot into the mountainside to crash and burn.

Using a mind, will and emotion paradigm, we see how these parts of the brain are centers for different contributions to healing. The mind centers in the thinking cap, holding the facts. Emotions center in the emotional brain, holding experiences as vivid emotional memories. Our will plays a part as we choose to work or not to work in concert with God toward healing. God desires to heal this destructive cycle within us. We can cooperate with God and allow Him to expose and then to heal our sins, wounds and lies under the blanket of God's grace. Without accepting His grace, we will have difficulty experiencing the peace that passes understanding. Jesus said, "Peace I leave with you. My [own] peace I now give and bequeath to you. Not as the world gives, do I give to you.

Do not let your hearts be troubled, neither let them be afraid. [Stop allowing yourselves to be agitated and disturbed; and do not permit yourselves to be fearful and intimidated and cowardly and unsettled.]" (John 14:27)

**7. Journal your thoughts and feelings about any childhood wounds you feel comfortable remembering.**

## God's Sanctification Program

Our current society has countless recovery programs: recovery from drugs, anorexia, rage, overeating, obsessive/compulsive disorders, overspending, gambling, pornography, and the list goes on. God invites us to His true recovery program; recovery through a new start after we shared in the fall of Adam and Eve. He wants us to know His love: to experience His peace that passes understanding, the joy of the Lord, His Sabbath rest, healthy relationships and emotional stability in His ability on our behalf. We experience this magnificent love through His grace.

God's recovery program is called His Sanctification Program. Sanctification is defined in Harper's Bible Dictionary as "making holy or consecrating a place, thing, or person to God." At our new birth God sets us apart from the world system into His Sanctification Program. He begins to make our new life in Christ a reality for us. God's Sanctification Program has no vengeance in it. He compassionately works for us on our behalf. He heals the wounds, replaces toxic lies with living truths, and forgives our sins. We may not yet be aware that a particular way of thinking or acting is harmful to us and others; but because of God's merciful love He will not let us continue hurting others and creating our own pain. Even if we crash and burn, God is there to pick us up and continue healing us if we choose with our wills to allow Him to do so.

Once we receive a new life in Christ, we need time to grow, to actualize our new life in Christ. This is like learning to play golf. You may take beginning golf lessons, but it takes time to learn all you need to know and do. Drs. Cloud and Townsend espouse, "Wherever you find the law of God + the grace of God + time in balance, the real Jesus is present." Time is something Christians don't seem to factor into their personal equation for change. We need time to grow and heal.

God sees us through the eyes of compassion and provides what we need. If He did not already know that we need healing there would be no Sanctification Program. In this program, God is in the transforming business as Romans 12:2 says, "Do not be conformed to this world but be transformed by the renewal of your mind so that you may prove for yourself what is the good and acceptable and perfect will of God [that which is perfect in God's sight for us]." As we are diligent (2 Peter 1:5) to place ourselves in various activities such as church, Bible studies, prayer groups, Christian therapy, Bible reading, discipleship groups, mentoring groups and church programs geared towards emotional healing, God will do the transforming.

Will God really heal us? Yes! Philippians 2:13 states, "Not in your own strength, for it is God who is all the while effectually at work in you [energizing and creating in you the power and desire], both to will and to work for His good pleasure and satisfaction and delight." If we choose not to partner with God to expose our sins, wounds and toxic lies, He will let us come to the end of ourselves. We inadvertently create the painful consequences of our actions, attitudes, and beliefs that run contrary to God's will. The pain can be redemptive, bringing us to repentance: changing our minds about the direction we are going and looking to God for change.

Will you participate in God's sanctification program? What if you could start today accepting as fact that the Holy Spirit came into your soul (mind, will and emotions) to save you from yourself? What if you could truly grasp the reality that God loves you and wants to rescue you from yourself? What if you accepted that sanctification is God's process of setting you free from your sinful self? What if we accept that painful wake-up call when we crash and burn as a gift from God showing where He wants to heal us? What if we choose this sometimes painful process, welcoming God as He brings to our attention issues that need His healing? What if we could stop judging and condemning ourselves for needing God's help? We would grow in God's grace, and God's peace and love: our hearts would soar.

## In Summary

Because we fear being exposed for who we believe we are and we think we are not good enough for God to love us, we judge and condemn ourselves. In this fragile state of fear, our pride keeps us from admitting to others, ourselves and to God that we need help. We try to be strong and to earn love from God by presenting a false self to the world, one that looks successful, but covers a wounded, ashamed real self.

This false self is too proud to need or accept God's grace, so our relationship with God and with our real self stays stuck in confusion and pain. We wonder why God's love seems so far away, and many Christians either fall away from the church in despair or just keep on keeping on enduring life. Day after day, they pretend to be okay with God and with themselves. Others are discouraged. Disillusioned and angry, they feel they can never be good enough to be loved by God, so they act out their pain in unhealthy ways. We need to experience God's love.

God made a way to graciously accept us into His forever family, to give us a new identity and to heal our wounds, lies and sinful ways. We came into His family just as we are; however, because He loves us so very much, He will not leave us just as we are. He makes us anew, walking with us into His reality for us in Christ. God is removing us from the profane and the secular, and consecrating us to Himself with His Sanctification Program.

We can partner with God and choose to accept that we are not adequate and admit that we do need a savior. We can take ownership of our sins and our wounds and be transparent with ourselves and God without judgment. When God comes in, He forgives our sins, heals our wounds, overcomes our fears, and transforms our self-talk with His truth. We begin to experience His love as His grace transforms our hearts.

Take time to review your journal answers to the chapter questions. Talk with a trusted friend or counselor about your Sanctification Program: what concerns you; what confuses you; and what questions you have.

# CHAPTER 2

# GOD ESTEEM

## *Connecting with the Heart of God*

### *Trusting*

I crept along with the mass of cars surrounding me. I couldn't help raging, thinking how badly this mess was wearing on my engine. I stared back at the red, blinking lights. My lids fell as my head dropped between white knuckles. I jumped, noticing someone in my car. Relaxing to my right was Jesus Christ! I was actually embarrassed to admit it, but I had totally forgotten He was with me.

I remembered back at home, eight years old, praying to receive Him in Mrs. Boyd's Sunday school class. Words sliced through my thoughts, "Mind if I drive?" He asked. "Oh, I'm fine." I straightened up, gripping the wheel with confidence as I endured another traffic light. He smiled patiently, looking ahead. We crawled along.

With each exit we passed, weariness began to weigh more heavily on my face. "Oh, go ahead. I guess I could use the break." Through the miles, I *tried not to stare, but I could not help coveting His strength. And that face of His was so accepting. He glanced over at me with a knowing look as I forced my eyes ahead. I blushed, realizing what a control freak He must think I am. With a deep breath I finally stretched out my legs, "This is great!" I confessed. "Why did it take so long for me to hand it over to Him?" I wondered.*

*As we merged onto the interstate, He suggested that I might want to enjoy the ride home. I agreed to rest my eyes for just a minute. Jumping, I found myself startled again! "Why am I lying in the passenger seat of my own car?" I flashed a dazed look at the driver. I remembered Him and felt at ease. Discreetly, I wiped the drool from the corner of my grin with a realization that there may be hope for me after all.*

*By Ashley Wille*

In the first chapter, we saw how easily we can frustrate and even nullify the grace of God in our lives. We often do this by judging and condemning ourselves, believing lies and by trying to earn love and acceptance. In this chapter we will see how much God esteems His children and why we must consider loving ourselves as God does. In order to not confuse loving ourselves with secular self-esteem, I have coined the term *God Esteem*." Christians are to have a strong *God Esteem*.

## A Relationship with God through Jesus

Through His death and resurrection, Jesus made a love relationship possible between God and each one of us. He modeled for us what a real relationship with God looks like. Our relationship with our Father is to be patterned after and resemble the love relationship Jesus has with His Father. Just as Jesus understands who He is in the Father, we are to know and live out of who we are in Christ. Just as Jesus knew He walked in God's favor, we are to know we walk in God's favor, not because we are perfect as Jesus is perfect, but because Jesus lived out our perfection for us. And just as Jesus accepted for Himself God's love, joy, peace, patience, kindness, long suffering, grace, mercy, directions, and acceptance, we are to accept these gifts for ourselves. Jesus and God have an intimate love relationship with one another. We too are to have an intimate love relationship with the Father, the Son, and the Holy Spirit, as we too are God's children.

Jesus did not fear His Father. Their relationship was one of mutual love. Too many Christians think of God as a Judge under the Law of the Old Covenant. We are under a New Covenant. This New Covenant is of Grace, with loving, merciful provisions for all who will come to God in faith through Jesus Christ. When the Bible says we are to fear God, it is a reverential awe and respect for who He is. As Christians we are to not be afraid of God as if He was trying to hurt us. We are God's blood-bought children and He is our Father. God went to great lengths to adopt us. Let us, as Christians, not see Him as a God of vengeance against us any more. Unbelievers are under God's eternal judgment until they become believers in His Son. We, however, are believers and are no longer under God's wrath.

1. **Read 1 John 4:18, and journal your feelings and thoughts as to what it says personally to you. In light of this reading, what is reality for you as an individual?**

## A Relationship where God Esteems His Children

If we want to understand more of the relationship God wants us to have with us, we must look at Scripture.

43

"What then shall we say to [all] this? If God is for us, who [can be] against us? [Who can be our foe, if God is on our side?]" (Romans 8:31). Our answer to this question posed in Scripture often seems to be, "I am against myself." Through my experience of my own war with myself and those of my clients, God showed me how very special you and I are to Him. God is for us, and none can stand against us because *He loves us*!

The spark of His love toward us shines early in Scripture. In Genesis 1:26 God says, "Let us (Father, Son and Holy Spirit) make mankind in our image, after Our likeness..." God could have fashioned us any way He wanted, yet He chose to form us *in His own image*. He had a purpose for fashioning us after Himself. He is love, and He extends His love to us and then through us to others (1 John 4:8, 11) as an expression of Himself.

Not only did God choose to create us in His image; but, in love, He personally and delicately hand-knit each person's unique being with all its complexities. "For you did form my inward parts; You did knit me together in my mother's womb." (see Psalm 139:13-16, Exodus 4:11, Psalm 100:3b) How special we are: the very essence of our being has been fashioned by the Master's hands! We are specifically and *uniquely designed* in all respects: our personality, our physical characteristics, our interests, our IQ, and so much more. We may not be perfect physically, yet behind His distinctive design He has an exclusive plan based on His will and how He formed us. He has a unique mission for us to fulfill within our sphere of influence during our lifetime.

The Psalms show us how God thinks of us. "How precious and weighty are your thoughts to me O God! How vast is the sum of them! If I could count them they would be more in number than the sand." (Psalm 139:17-18) Truly, God's thoughts toward you are "precious and weighty." This means He *esteems* you, *values* you, and considers you *precious.* "For He knows our frame, He earnestly remembers and imprints [on His heart] that we are dust." (Psalm 103:13-14) Have you ever held a butterfly your hand? Did you notice the dusty wings begin to disintegrate when you touch them? Like these small creatures, our humanness is fragile in God's economy. He lovingly remembers this during our sojourn on this earth and desires to enter into our lives to support, strengthen, guide and love us.

David treasured God's thoughts toward him, exclaiming, "Because Your loving kindness is better than life, my lips shall praise You." (Psalm 63) We pass through difficult seasons, just as David did. During times of trouble and suffering, David praised God and learned to receive God's love as His life. Why could he do this? Because he knew how God *treasured* him by giving him lovingkindness.

God says to us, "You are a chosen race, a royal priest-hood, a dedicated nation, [God's] own purchased, special people, that you may set forth the wonderful deeds and display the virtues and perfections of Him who called you out of darkness into His marvelous light." (1 Peter 4:9) God says we are *chosen* by Him. We are a *special* people to him as He has appointed us as a royal priesthood.

These verses help us begin to see how highly God esteems us. We are well made, as we are made in His image. He thinks good thoughts toward us. If God thinks we are special, ought we also to think of ourselves as special? "In the same way that the one who loves God should love his brother also." (1 John 4:19-21) Since you and I as fellow Christians are called to love our brothers and sisters, can we not also value ourselves as one of those brothers and sisters; and esteem ourselves in the same way God wants us to love others?

**2. How would your life be different if you were to esteem yourself as God does? Journal your thoughts and feelings about this.**

## *The Royal Rule*

As I was reading my Bible one morning, I read a truth about God and His love that would change me forever. This truth stopped me from continuing to wound myself with my negative self-talk. I believe what I found is a significant biblical truth often overlooked in our Christian teachings. Without knowing this missing truth, I had continued to cover up the real me as I silently judged myself. I took seriously this missing piece, and it eventually equipped me to come out of hiding and be authentic with God, myself and others. This missing piece is rarely spoken of in churches.

The missing truth is as critical for the believer as John 3:16 is for the unbeliever. John 3:16 conveys the gospel, the Good News, in as few words as possible, yet keeps the integrity of the whole counsel of God. *God loves you. God sent His Son. If you believe in His Son, you will not perish but have eternal life.* This verse gives the non-believer the choice of eternal separation from God or eternal life in God's presence.

The missing truth I found (in Matthew 22:34-40) is as critical for the believer as John 3:16 is for the unbeliever. This passage is often called The Royal Rule. Acting upon the Royal Rule can give us the capacity to experience God's love and to share that love with others. These verses are the key to moving from internal conflict to a joy-filled connection with life and with God. Just as we share John 3:16 with unbelievers, if I could only select one scripture to share with a believer, it would be Matthew 22:34-40. Jesus says:

> *34Now when the Pharisees heard that He had silenced [muzzled] the Sadducees, they gathered together. 35And one of their number, a lawyer, asked Him a question to test Him. 36Teacher, which kind of commandment is great and important in the law? 37And He replied to him, You shall love the Lord your God with all your heart and with all your soul and with all your mind [intellect].38 This is the great [most important principal] and the first commandment. 39And the second is like it: You shall love your neighbor as [you do] yourself. 40These two commandments sum up and upon them depend all the Law and the Prophets.*

Jesus tells us these two laws are preeminent over all other laws. The first law tells us to love God. The second law tells us to love others as we love ourselves. Look closely at these two laws and you will find Jesus commanding us to love three entities; first and above the others, we are to love God; secondly, to love ourselves; and thirdly, to love others. Only two of these three are generally addressed in Christian circles: God and others.

Leaving out *loving yourself* is a grave oversight. As Jesus goes on to say; "If you love God, and love others as you love yourself, you will be fulfilling all the law and the prophets." Harper's Bible Dictionary says, "Everything hangs upon the law of love; take away this, and all falls to the ground and comes to nothing." "For the fulfilling of the law is love and the end of the law is love." (Romans 13:10) The Christian faith is about love being preeminent in all facets of our lives. "Love never fails." (1Timothy 1:5)

Receiving salvation by grace, new believers come into the church with a new love relationship with God. Usually they are encouraged to go out and love others in ministry. I contend we cannot give ourselves away in love unless we have a self that is loved. If we block God's grace for living, we will not experience His love in our lives. Jesus had a perfect self and a perfect love relationship with the Father. Jesus was loved, and He chose to give Himself away in love on our behalf. It is essential for us to know who we are in Christ and what we have already been given to help us in our pilgrimage in this world. It is very much worth doing the internal work necessary which opens us up to the grace and love of God.

**3. Personalize and write out the Royal Rule. What are your spontaneous thoughts and feelings about loving yourself? Journal how you experience yourself in light of the three relationships of the Royal Rule.**

### *God Esteem vs. Self Esteem*

I would select the Royal Rule to share with a believer because it covers all the relationships in our lives (God, others and self). We need to remember God is love. (1 John 4:8) Relationship with us is so important to Him! Yet down through the ages, and even today, self-abasement is seen as a desirable spiritual attitude, suggesting that to think of oneself as a worthwhile person is sinful and prideful.

The phrase *loving yourself* seems to smack of secular psychology, and this concerns many theologians. I believe for every truth God gives us, Satan skews and presents it in the form of a poisonous, toxic lie. In a continuing education class I attended, the instructor made a snide remark about Christianity. She said that Christians use the acronym J-O-Y: *Jesus* first, *Others* second and *Yourself* last. Instead, she thought that (speaking from a secular self esteem) it should be *Self* first and *Others* last I quickly considered what she was saying. God seemed to speak to me, "When you put Me first, you are also putting yourself first because your life is in my hands. Since you are now my child, our lives are intrinsically intertwined, so you and I are inseparable." This teacher derided Christians by intimating we should beware of Christianity because it would subjugate and keep them down. Because of this misperception I do not use the acronym J-O-Y. Too many people distort the true meaning of it and use it to oppress themselves.

When Jesus says to love yourself, He is not suggesting we exhibit a grandiose self-love, one that puts another down for the purpose of exalting oneself. Nor is He referencing the *me* generation attitude which says, "It's all about me." Jesus is not encouraging self-promotion. Neither is He addressing the New Age spirituality with its emphasis on being the best you that you can be. He is not even talking about having a good self esteem. Healthy self love grows from how God loves and esteems us. If God loves and esteems me, I should love and esteem myself in the same way. As I grow in Christ I like myself more and more. I love the new creation God is forming in me.

Secular self esteem is inconsistent with the gospel. It is not our goal when learning to love ourselves. Secular psychology helps the client become stronger in their flesh, in order to strengthening this self esteem. Yet becoming stronger in ourselves is in direct opposition to the Word of God. Christianity teaches we have the inability to live out God's directives. This causes us to turn to God for His strength and His ability, which He gives us through the indwelling of the Holy Spirit. God Esteem frees us to embrace the reality of our inadequacy yet at the same time to embrace the truth that we are made new by God. We have His strength and His identity through the Holy Spirit within us.

4. **Journal your understanding and experience of secular self esteem. How does God Esteem differ? Why is secular self esteem in opposition to God Esteem? What are your personal thoughts and feelings about that difference?**

## Three Distinct Relationships

Using Matthew 23: 34-40 as our guide, we discover there are three distinct relationships we are to attend to as Christians: loving God, esteeming ourselves and esteeming others. It is simple to understand a two-way relationship with God. In our relationship with God we talk to Him about our lives, confessing our sins, asking for help, and praising Him for His provision for us. We grow in love for Him, and we purpose to obey Him. His relationship with us is one of unconditional love. He tells us in His Word all He has already given us as joint heirs with Jesus! Through the power of the Holy Spirit, He leads us, guides us, teaches us, convicts us, and gives us insight regarding who He is and who we are. He directs our everyday lives.

We can also understand having a two-way relationship with others. I have a relationship with you and you have a relationship with me. Easy! But how do I have a two-way relationship with myself? That is harder to understand. It can be difficult to conceive of my having a relationship with myself and in turn, myself having a relationship with me. Each of us does have a relationship with themselves, however. It may be a good relationship or it may be a poor relationship but it is a relationship nonetheless. When I ask a client, "How is your relationship with yourself?" without hesitation, the most common answer is, "Oh, I am really tough on myself." Each person seems to know what I am asking. Now who is being tough on whom?

The answer to this question is explained in different ways. Secular psychology uses a metaphor: the present self is berating and wounding their own inner child. The one doing the berating is the person living at the present time. The person living in the present is bullying the wounded self from the past, which is called the *inner child* because the wounds happen in childhood but remain within the person. There is no real inner child, but the picture helps people see what they are doing to themselves and helps them take responsibility for taking care of the wounded parts of themselves. From a Christian's perspective I would say the flesh of the present person is wounding the unhealed parts of the self.

Most Christians are unaware of the effects their harsh relationship with themselves has on their mental and spiritual health. We keep ourselves anxious, scared, defeated, and depressed. We do to ourselves what we want no one else to do to us. If we said the same things to another that we say to ourselves, we would call it sin. Isn't this sin against ourselves? Do we not sin against ourselves and further damage the wounded part of ourselves? We hammer a wedge between God and ourselves, separating ourselves from receiving His love.

**5. Do you have a relationship with yourself? How do you know? Journal about what that relationship is like.**

### *Three Facets of Self*

As God's children we want intimate connectedness to God, not distance from God. Too often we experience that our thoughts, feelings, and actions are inconsistent with the persons we desire to be as Christians. We must understand this inconsistency if we want to change it. Three facets of our personhood are described in Scripture. One part, which we

will call the New Self, loves the Lord so very much and is so
excited about new life in Christ. But there is another part we
experience as duplicitous and double-minded; as quickly as
a knee jerk, this second part will sin. We will call this second
part the Flesh Self. Finally, there seems to be a third part that
sabotages us: the Wounded Self.

### 1) The New Self Facet

The first facet of ourselves we are to appreciate and love
is the new creature God created at our new birth. The new self
now has a new life and a new identity in Christ. "Therefore
if anyone is in Christ, he is a new creature; the old things
have passed away; behold, all things have become new." (2
Corinthians 5:17). The moment we receive Christ, spiritual
and emotional growth begins. Our dead spirits are quickened (made alive) by God and then sealed with the Holy
Spirit. Scripture tells us God has replaced our hearts of stone
with a new heart. In fact, Colossians 2:11 says, "In Him,
also you were circumcised with a circumcision not made
with hands, but in a [spiritual] circumcision [performed by]
Christ by stripping off the body of flesh [the whole corrupt,
carnal nature with its passions and lusts.]" We now have a
new identity. This new identity comes with many blessings
attached to it.

### 2) The Flesh Self Facet

John speaks of our flesh as having appetites triggered by
the world system. "For all that is in this world, the lust of
the flesh [craving for sensual gratification], and the lust of
the eyes [greedy longings of the mind], and the pride of life
[assurance in one's own resources or the stability of earthly
things], these do not come from the Father but are from this
world." (1 John 2:16) God's power through the Holy Spirit is

offered to overcome our flesh, which is not our literal physical bodies, but the part of us that gained power because of sin. Romans 8:3b states, "Sending His own Son in the guise of sinful flesh and as an offering for sin, God condemned sin in the flesh [subdued, overcame, deprived it of its power] over all who accept the sacrifice." Jesus delivers us from the power our flesh self. Romans 6

Even though the flesh is now deprived of its power in our lives, we may not experience this reality. Often from a lack of awareness or wrong teaching, our flesh continues to control our lives. We must believe God regarding our flesh. Our flesh self is rendered powerless, dead because of Christ! This does not mean we will never sin again, but we can overcome temptations to let the flesh self lead us into sin. We remind ourselves of God's truth in the place of temptation. We remember that our flesh has been deprived of its power over us. But when we do sin, as we sometimes will, we claim this truth: "If we confess our sins, God is faithful and just to forgive us." (1 John 1:9) God has covered us at the point of temptation to sin and after we do sin. Praise God!

## 3) The Wounded Self Facet

Intertwined with our flesh self is the wounded self, the third facet of ourselves. We often wrestle with this part that holds painful wounds from others and often from ourselves, too. Many are childhood wounds, results of sins against us when we were young. This wounded self may have experienced rejection; personal failures; anger and rage vented on an undeserving, unprotected child; or the emotional, physical or sexual abuse of others.

In the same way a pain shoots into the body when a tender physical wound is jabbed; when the wounded self is jabbed, when the wounded self is poked, temptation triggers the flesh self to lash out at others or to lash in on the self.

Just as we were wounded in different circumstances and in different ways, these triggers will be different for each of us. For instance, a scent can be a trigger. When an uncle wearing a particular type of aftershave lotion has molested his young niece, if she encounters any man wearing the same aftershave, she may have a strong negative reaction to this other person. Until she understands what is happening to her, she may feel rage or depression and not know why. A man she meets may be someone who could be a fine husband for her, but if he wears this aftershave, she probably would do everything she could do to avoid him. Sadly, a potential relationship would be sabotaged because of the effects of her wounds.

I had this kind of experience in graduate school. I was and still am a disaster at math. As a child, recognizing I could not do math at the level of my elementary school classmates filled me with humiliation, shame, and hate toward myself. I was so dumb! I carried this label with me as an adult. I even majored in elementary education for my undergraduate degree because I would only have to take one math course: the theory of arithmetic.

When I wanted to become a counselor, I went on to graduate school. I knew the degree requirements included a statistics course. I was terrified! The school offered a prep course to help people like me pass statistics. I signed up immediately. One day in this class several of us had to complete a particular statistics problem on the blackboard in front of the rest of the class. As I walked to the blackboard, fear gripped me and my mind went blank. At forty-three years of age, I was suddenly crying uncontrollably. What was happening? I had traveled back to the wounded part of me and my wounded self had become again the nine-year-old little girl alone at the blackboard hearing her third grade peers snicker at her failure.

Fortunately, my graduate statistics professor was also a practicing psychologist. She understood what was happening. She put her arm around me and we turned to face the small class. With her arm still around me, she took me to each student and asked me to look into his or her eyes. I was filled with shame, making this very difficult for me. But as I looked into each person's eyes, they told me how much they cared for me, understood my fear, and assured me this did not in any way cloud what they thought of me. God healed and freed me in that moment! Peace rushed in, surrounding that little girl with love and healing that shame-filled wound forever.

I now tell people without shame that I am not good in math and suggest that they might want to handle splitting the check for eight ladies at lunch. I speak grace towards myself and tell myself the truth. The truth is, "I am not good in math. But God in His unique plan for me did not equip me for math because He had other plans for my life. There are many things I can do and that I do very well." Shame keeps us hiding. When my shame wound was healed I had nothing to fear. With nothing to hide, we can be authentic with others and even laugh at ourselves.

6. **Take each of the three facets of yourself one by one and journal how you experience each of these in your everyday life. Which one or ones are you more familiar with and why?**

### *Embracing All Three Facets of Ourselves*

Although I have individually described these three facets of ourselves, we simultaneously experience them as three very different realities: our new nature, our flesh, and our wounds. They push and pull on us, and this clash in our minds and hearts creates what therapists call *cognitive disso-*

*nance* within us. If we do not understand what is happening, the dissonance we feel may make us wonder if we really are Christians.

God is aware we operate out of these three realities and desires we embrace and accept all three as He does; for this is the way of healing. The conflict we feel is resolved when we learn not to condemn ourselves, but to hold these three realities in tension. We have a new nature which grows stronger when we accept it as fact and nourish that new nature. Our flesh is still within us, but God has provided a way for us to control the flesh, not yielding to its desires (Romans 6). But our flesh still is a fact. Our wounds are real, too. They are a fact. In our Sanctification Program, God will pour on us His grace and love and progressively heal our wounds. As these three aspects of ourselves vie for first place within us, they cause conflict within us; that is a fact. God, through the Holy Spirit within us, teaches us and leads us to treat all aspects of ourselves with love and respect.

It is important to remember it is not what we are at the moment but whose we are and the direction we are going. We must remember that we belong to God; that He has promised to make us like His Son; and that His Son was tempted in every way that we are, yet without sin. (Hebrews 4:15) Understanding that God knows all this can help us relax and accept the tension of these three realities.

If we allow the Lord to build God Esteem into our lives we will accept God's grace and experience God's love. As God sets us free from the pain of our wounds, from our bondage to sins, and from the toxic lies we believe, little by little we become the person we have always wanted to be in Christ. A miracle takes place! As we collaborate with God, our conflicted lives become more joy-filled and peaceful than we could ever imagine. This is our goal in God's Sanctification Program. We give over our will, the sins of our flesh and our wounds to the Lord. God will remove our old ways of being and thinking in order to experience ourselves as God does with eyes of compassion and love.

So the question for you becomes, *what is reality?* Is reality the way we see and experience ourselves or the way God sees us? Your answer will determine the direction of your Christian walk. You will either be moving toward experiencing God's love and Sabbath rest or moving away from experiencing God's love by how you answer this question. (Hebrews 4:9).

**7. What would your daily life be like if you could embrace all three parts of yourself, knowing that God is not judging you but wanting to help you grow? Journal your thoughts and feelings about this.**

## My Journey to God Esteem

My personal journey from low self esteem to God Esteem began to take form twelve to fourteen years after I became a Christian. My war with God had ended when I became a Christian at age 30; however, my war with myself still raged.

I grew up as the only child of much older parents. My father was born in 1894, a product of the Victorian period. He was fifty-one when I was born. This may not seem unusual to you now with so many couples marrying later in life. But when I was growing up most people were married by the time they were in their early twenties. The Victorian culture from which he came was very different than the culture I experienced.

I was a compliant child, so I didn't mind the increased control he seemed to feel was proper. This may even appeal to some who have been emotionally or physically abused. As a counselor, I now understand that this kind of overprotection actually is a form of covert rejection, which is not physically or verbally displayed. Neither the parent nor the child may be aware that this is what is happening.

My parents made most of the decisions in my life. They decided what I would wear, who would be my friends, where I would go to high school and college, as well as choosing my college major. When a child is overprotected and the parents are making all the important decisions, the child has little opportunity or experience in making their own decisions. They grow up not knowing what they want out of life, what they need, or what they like and dislike. All those decisions have been made for them, so they have no idea how to make decisions. This overprotection gave me the impression that I was not capable of doing things for myself or making competent decisions. I believed I needed someone to do that for me. I needed someone strong in my life, because I must not be strong and wise enough by myself. This toxic lie began to direct my life.

The overprotected child does not have a healthy sense of self. Even as adults, they remain in a childlike state, a disorder known as *learned helplessness*. They have learned to be helpless. Learned helplessness played into my feelings of being less than others. I believed that others could do for themselves, but that I could not do for myself. As a young adult, I believed I needed someone to take care of me. As I look back on my life, I realize I was drawn to people who were seemingly strong and self-sufficient. So when it came time to pick a husband, I picked a seemingly strong, self-sufficient young man. It did not take long for me to discover that he would not allow me to attach my umbilical cord to him as I had been attached to my parents. I was furious! When I asked for advice, guidance, or direction, he would say, "Do what you want to do."

Some of you may be thinking, "Wow! It is so affirming to have a husband who gives you that freedom." And it is for many women. But freedom for me was not a gift. It was a terrifying nightmare. Freedom was the last thing I wanted since I inadvertently had learned to be helpless and expected to be cared for by others. I wanted to be told what to do and how to do it.

As a young wife, I raged for years because he was not there for me, giving direction and guidance. I felt dismissed, rejected, misunderstood, and not loved by him. I just knew he had the solutions for me and refused to share them with me. I told myself, "He is holding back. I am a poor orphan left on my own. Poor me! Why did I marry him?" There was nothing I had in and of myself to live life. I had never developed a self within. I knew I had a non-self that had to be hidden from everyone at all times. "Who am I?" I wondered. I was scared, hurt, and angry.

My daily life operated out of a vacuum, imitating others and trying to find myself. It was a terrifying, painful, and anxiety-producing lifestyle. What do you suppose my self-talk was like? Even though I did put my umbilical cord onto Jesus at age thirty, I continued with the negative self-talk that was so familiar. I made no connection between who God says I am in Christ and who I experienced myself to be each day. Rather than rejoicing in the new me, I belittled, put down, condemned, and judged myself constantly. I was at war with myself.

One day my Christian therapist asked me to put that part of myself, that part of me I so disliked, in the chair next to me and talk to that part. Surprisingly, out of my mouth came a deluge of derogatory comments. One comment I remember well, because as I spoke, tears began to trickle down my therapist's cheeks. She grieved as she heard me vent to myself and say, "I hate you. I hate you. I wish you were dead. If you were dead then I would be okay."

When I came home that day, I sat silently before the Lord. I knelt and told God what He already knew: I hate myself. What was I to do? I then asked for His forgiveness. I said, "I do not know how to love myself the way You love me; however, I trust You and the Holy Spirit to do that work in me. I do not want to continue to defile what You have glorified in Christ Jesus. Father, I believe I have been blocking Your grace by not being in agreement with You about myself."

That day I made a life-changing commitment to myself as assuredly as the day I made a life-changing commitment to Christ. I made a pledge to learn to respect and to love myself the way God does. This was the beginning of my emotional healing, allowing the love of God to flow into my wounded heart and soul. The war with myself would soon be over.

This hate was out of God's will. Awareness is the beginning of healing. I cannot go to God with something I do not know exists. Prior to this new awareness I was fodder for Satan because I did not know what he knew, that I hated myself. Without this knowledge he could adversely impact my life at any moment he chose by triggering all my neuroses. With awareness I could pray specifically, asking God to heal my estimation of myself and help me experience the reality of who I am in Christ. God began teaching me *God Esteem*.

9. **Do you identify with any of the elements in my story? Journal how and what you identify with. In what ways do you experience God Esteem? Or do you?**

## In Summary

As we come to the close of this chapter, we see that one-third of the Royal Rule is generally missing in our Christian teachings. This lack of understanding hinders our spiritual maturation as we find ourselves condemning and judging ourselves and those closest to us. Painful spiritual and emotional dissonance in the believer's heart becomes toxic, poisoning their family relationships, their work relationships, and even in their church family relationships.

As Jesus experienced His Father's love, He was able to share that love with others. Since we too are the beloved children of God, should we not also savor God's love and acceptance for ourselves as Jesus does and share it with others? Should we not learn to love and to respect ourselves the way God loves and respects Jesus and us, too, because of Jesus and His grace? Don't we owe it to ourselves and to God to accept all He has made available for us through the death of His Son on the cross?

God will, in fact, eternally keep us in His forever family. He wants us to acknowledge, embrace, and receive all His gifts. It was at great personal expense God made a way through Jesus to exalt us to such a grand position in Christ. Thus we honor God by accepting who God says we are in Christ.

It is time for a decision. Just as assuredly as the day you made a commitment to Jesus, God would like for you to make a commitment to yourself: a commitment to forgive yourself as He does; to have mercy on yourself, as He does; to speak with respect when addressing yourself, as He does; and to give yourself grace, instead of judgment, as He does. We are truly loving God and loving ourselves when we take Him at His word.

How may we begin to truly see ourselves? We might say, "I am an inadequate, faltering, sinful, wounded child of God with a new identity and all the benefits of a child of God. God is helping me to actualize and experience all I have been given by Him in Christ and through his Sanctification Program."

Let us wrap ourselves tightly in the robe of righteousness given to us by God and rest in who we are in Christ. We must work with God rather than against Him, remembering we are the temple of the Holy Spirit. Let us walk in agreement with

God and treat our temples with respect, compassion, acceptance, dignity, and love.

**Spend some quiet time journaling to God about where you are with the issue of your loving Him and trusting His goodness. If you are ready, ask Him to teach you how to love yourself as He loves you.**

# CHAPTER 3

# ANOTHER GOSPEL THAT IS NOT THE GOSPEL

## *Condemnation Or Grace?*

### *Through the Eyes of God*

*When I look in the mirror each morning, whom do I see? How do I feel about this person? What are my thoughts about myself looking back at me? Might I see myself through the eyes of a critical parent, or perhaps through the eyes of a disappointed teacher? Or through some difficult circumstances I have endured? In my distant thoughts I may hear God condemning me because I fail to live up to His law. I don't even live up to my own standards, for which I condemn myself. I sometimes hear others' voices scolding me and condemning me as well, and sometimes I agree with them.*

*Someone please help me escape this cycle of condemnation!*

*When I neglect to discover God's real thoughts toward me, a false and unnecessary distance is expe-*

*rienced between God and me. It is a distance that He would prefer not exist. I tend to think God's thoughts of me are similar to my own thoughts of me. However, unlike my thoughts, God's thoughts of me are refreshingly high and uplifting! He holds nothing at all against me, but has absolute favor toward me! God has great interest in me experiencing this truth, so much that He personally made a way for me through His Son, Jesus. With a willing and child-like heart, I need only to receive.*

*By Ashley Wille*

A chapter focusing on condemnation may seem unusual since we are targeting experiencing God's love. Experiencing grace in all areas of our lives is the key to experiencing God's love. Discerning what the Gospel of Jesus Christ *is* and what the gospel of Jesus Christ *is not* is critical for our spiritual growth. Too many Christians are living according to a false gospel, what Paul calls, "another gospel that is not the gospel." (Galatians 1) Because we do not understand what the real Gospel is, we continue to condemn and judge ourselves.

The word *gospel* means good news. Operating out of a law mindset is not the good new of Jesus Christ. As 2 Corinthians 3:6 states, "the letter of the law kills..." Keeping the law, which is legalism, cannot lead to divine redemption or to being kept in the faith. Many people walk away from the Christian faith because they reject this false gospel, this legalism, believing it is the real gospel.

## The Law is Not the Good News of Jesus Christ

*Law* can be defined as *rules of conduct of any organized society, however simple or small, that are enforced by threat of punishment if they are violated.* (Columbia Encyclopedia) A nation's law is a system for enforcing rules of conduct which have been designed to allow people to function in an efficient manner within their region of residence. When the law is broken, agencies such as city police, state troopers, and the FBI enforce the law with punishment. Without law is anarchy. Even within a family, which is a small organized society, rules of conduct prevent anarchy.

God's Law functions in this same way. We have a healthy and safe environment for living when we follow God's rules of conduct. It is like a gated neighborhood, where we can run free and enjoy life without the chaos and dangers that run rampant outside the community gates. God in His wisdom and concern for us gives these directives to protect us with boundary lines for our safety, helping us understand there is danger lurking outside of God's Law. In a similar way, loving parents set appropriate boundaries for the safety and protection of their children.

Bob George, the author of *Classic Christianity*, coined the phrase "the Ministry of Condemnation" as a name describing the intention of God's Law. What is this Ministry of Condemnation? We are driven by a force within us called our *sin nature* to put our hairy toe across God's boundary lines. When we cross the boundary line, we sin, and we experience consequences under the Law. Going past God's boundaries ultimately creates a crisis for us because we find ourselves in painful places and situations we never thought we would go. Like a father who loves his child, He offers us the real gospel. He wants to give us a new nature that desires to stay within His boundaries. Bob George labels this the "Ministry of Acceptance."

**1. How would you explain the Ministry of Condemnation? What does this say to you?**

# Four Purposes of the Law

When we understand the purposes of the Law, we can know the real gospel based on grace, and we can forsake the false gospel based on the Law. The Apostle Paul wrestled with his confusion between the Law, his sin nature and his new identity in Christ. *What is the Law? How does the Law impact our propensity to sin?* Paul struggles with and answers these questions. (Romans 7:7-25) The ministry of condemnation worked in our lives prior to becoming a Christian.

### The Law Defines Sin

The first purpose of the Law is to define what constitutes sin. God's rules of conduct point out what is acceptable, and what is dangerous or harmful. Paul says if we had no laws we would have no knowledge of sin. (Romans 4:15) We recognize sin as breaking God's boundaries.

### The Law Shows Us Our Sin

The second purpose of the Law is to point out sin in our lives. When we know God's rules of conduct (which are holy, righteous, protective and good), we are accountable for keeping them. At this point we begin to see how far short we come from God's perfection. *Sin* is a Greek term used in archery that means *to miss the mark*, or the bull's-eye on the target. To be in God's presence, Jesus said we are, "To be perfect as My Father is perfect." (Mathew 5:48). We are to hit the bull's-eye of keeping the Law. When we miss this mark, we sin.

Why is sin of interest to God? The Bible says God is holy, the epitome of perfection and purity. Hebrews 12:29 says, "For our God is indeed a consuming fire." Though difficult to understand, our holy God cannot be in the presence of sin (imperfection). If we were to come into His presence prior to our accepting Christ who took away our sins, we would immediately be consumed by the flaming fire of His holiness (perfection). As long as we insist on carrying our own sin, we may be His creations, but we are not His children. Once we accept that Jesus has the legal right to carry our sins and He takes them away, we can enter into His presence without condemnation.

This awareness of our need for perfection begins early in life. By the age of three children think in terms of good and bad. Labeling ourselves bad seems to come naturally to us. If the Ministry of Acceptance, the true gospel of grace, is not presented and received, our hearts can become hardened, denying the reality of sin, believing there are no boundaries and there is no evil or God. Or if our hearts are soft toward God, but we do not understand the true gospel, we can descend into intense condemnation, depression and guilt.

I was a good example of a heart softened toward God, but without the true gospel of grace. As a young preteen, I cheated on a math test and was caught, creating a painful ordeal at school and at home. Ironically, I denied I cheated to my parents and they believed me and stood up for me. This made my pain far worse than it already was. Up until that age I cannot remember feeling guilty. I experienced fear of punishment but not guilt. One night after the turmoil settled down, I was in my bed thinking about what I had done: cheated and then lied to my parents, two sins. Deceiving my parents haunted me. They believed my deception. I remember the moment a deep sense of guilt overwhelmed me. The feeling was actually visceral. My organs felt twisted and assaulted as if I had been punched in the stomach. The

Ministry of Condemnation slipped into my room that night and took me down for the count.

The count lasted for years. The guilt of deceit followed me wherever I went. The pain hardly ever left my awareness. The Ministry of Condemnation had me is its grip. The unconscious way I tried to resolve the pain was to never lie again. "This is good. She learned her lesson," you might say. What happened, however, was beyond true conviction. If I never lie again, I reasoned, then I would be protected from ever feeling that kind of pain again. Notice my motivation, to be perfect in this area of my life so as to be free of pain.

An example of my behavior shows how this worked out for me. Let's say I bumped into you and admired your lovely violet sweater. When talking with another friend later in the day I might say, "I saw Susie today and she looked great in her purple sweater." Later I remember it was really violet. A deep painful depression would overtake me, because I had lied. I would feel the same feelings of emotional pain I felt that night in my bed. Every detail from then on had to be perfect or else the horrific pain would overtake me.

The *Ministry of Condemnation* hit me hard. I knew no way to get out from under it. I confessed over and over again to God with no sense of release. The obsessive feelings lasted intensely for at least five years until I was able to suppress it. Fear of that pain resurfacing haunted me until I received Jesus at age thirty. Not only did guilt haunt me but a greater and even more insidious entity entered my life — shame. My belief about myself became "I am a bad person. If others know how bad I am, they will scorn me, harass me, shame me, and reject me." I went to Sunday school and church every week. We learned historical facts, but our inner lives were never addressed except to say, "If you have bad thoughts in your mind, it's as good as doing the bad thing you are thinking." Sunday school facts and surface talk were all I received at my church. I was still a sinner without hope.

### The Law Brings Condemnation

The third purpose of the Law is to show us there is no way for us to fix our own sin nature. I knew right from wrong but I seemed to be drawn to do things I knew would push me down further into guilt and depression. I didn't know that when we find ourselves ensnared and doing what we do not want to do, we are caught in a sin cycle. Just like me, Paul was plagued, bewildered, and confused by this sin cycle trap. (Romans 7) Having knowledge of what is right and wrong, Paul continued to be trapped by doing just the opposite of what he desired. He would sin (miss the mark of perfection), seemingly against his own will. Paul then describes how he found himself at war with himself. In his mind a moral law tells him right from wrong and in his inner being there is a law of nature, a sin nature that wars against his mind and causes him to do things he knows are wrong and does not want to do. This forceful dynamic wages war against his desire to do good. Or, as Paul describes it, there is a sin principle at work within him. He neither has control of this force, nor can he fix himself. His sin nature controls him. He even goes so far as to say, "I am subject to its insistent demands." (Romans 7:21) Paul is imprisoned by this sin nature that lives within him. It has control of him. The Ministry of Condemnation has done its work. Paul is condemned with no way to escape.

2.  **I find that trying to appear and to present ourselves as "having it all together" is an obsession of our culture. Journal your thoughts on this. Describe ways you try to cover up the real you.**

### *The Law Drives Us to God*

The fourth purpose of the Law is to bring us face to face with the reality of our human sin nature, with the hope that we will accept God's solution for our sin. We need God to fix our sin nature with the gospel of grace. Can you identify with this force that seems to hold you back from doing what you know you could or should do? Ever try losing weight and then try continuing to hold that perfect weight? We can all think of ways we see the force of our sin nature. When we are convinced of our own sin and convinced there is no way out of the predicament, a humbling reality sinks in: I really do fall short of God's requirements for fellowship with Him. I am a sinner (I miss the mark of perfection). I am imperfect; I don't and I can't measure up to the standard of a holy God. I am inadequate and I cannot fix my problem. Help!

James 2:10 sums up our dilemma: "For whoever keeps the whole law and yet stumbles in one point, he has become guilty of all." "Well, just great; God! You give us Your law. We try to measure up and keep Your law, and then You say that if I stumble in one point, I'm guilty of all. I'm in a Catch-22. You have me checkmated. What am I to do?"

3. **Explain the Four Purposes of the Law and what they mean for you.**

4. **At what age were you aware of right and wrong? Journal your memories of what happened in your family when you did the wrong thing. Was there any grace shown when you did wrong? Explain.**

5. **Journal how your spiritual journey to the Lord relates or does not relate to each of the four purposes of the Law.**

# Only Three Alternatives

How do we approach God? Do we approach Him with a mindset based on the Law or a mindset based on grace? A Law mindset and a grace mindset are opposing paradigms. They cannot be mixed. Only three alternatives are possible for being acceptable to approach our holy God.

## *Alternative 1: Live by the Law*

Man tries to make himself acceptable to God by the Law. The Law says, "If you do such and such then I will accept you."

Based only on keeping the Law, this alternative is legalism. It says, "If you keep your end of the bargain, then I will keep mine. If you don't, I will reject you." There is no room for grace. The Law measures your performance. The Law becomes an external standard or ritual that must be performed or adhered to in order to be acceptable. Judaism and Islam both operate from a system of laws offering God's blessings or curses according to how well you live up to the commands.

Our legal system illustrates a law mindset. Very little grace is provided in the law, and it does not take into account the motivation of the heart. You must do what the law says. If you do not obey the law, you will be judged guilty and you will suffer the penalty attached to breaking the law. We occasionally see someone who is trapped by a *letter of the law* mindset which completely disregards motivation and focuses only on the specific details prescribed by the law. I remember seeing on the evening news a woman arrested for speeding. She jumped out of the car yelling, "My husband has had a heart attack! I have to get to the hospital!" A heart attack may call for some grace in penalty for exceeding the speed limit. Instead of grace, her strong overreaction was rewarded by the policeman handcuffing her and taking her to the police station. According to letter of the law, she was a dangerous offender.

My husband is an attorney. His legal training taught him to ask closed-ended questions such as, "Where were you the night of the crime on the 25th of May at 11:00 P.M.?" When on the witness stand the witness must answer with facts only. There is no room for "let me explain." Under the Law, facts are facts. In great contrast, I was trained as a licensed professional counselor to ask open-ended questions such as, "What is it about how your father treats you that you do not like?" This type of question is designed to get to the heart of the person and their motivation. As a lawyer, my husband is seeking facts under the law. As a counselor, I focus on heart issues, seeking to understand motivations behind facts and actions. A person living by the Law would only see a legal perspective, seeking to live by the letter of the Law.

## *Alternative 2: Saved by Grace, Live by the Law*

In this second alternative, man seeks to be made acceptable to God by a hybrid of the Law and grace. In it, we understand being saved by grace but then live by the Law. This is not Christianity and is not a real alternative, but sends two conflicting messages and creates internal conflict. Subtly a false gospel that is not the true gospel creeps into our faith, saying: Jesus-plus-something-else causes God to accept us. It could be Jesus-plus-going-to-Church-every-Sunday. Too many evangelicals live from this false gospel, robbed of the truth of God's love. We think we understand grace but we find ourselves back under the Law, in futility trying to measure up. The internal conflict rages and keeps us under the Ministry of Condemnation. Because of this misconception of Christianity, I have written this book.

### *Alternative 3: Saved by Grace, Live by Grace*

In the final alternative, man is made acceptable to God by His grace alone. Grace says, "If you do what I ask, then I will love and accept you. If you don't do what I ask, I will still love and accept you because you have accepted Jesus' payment of the penalty for your sin." Grace is based on God's performance on our behalf, not our performance on His behalf. Grace is something God does for us in spite of our inability to measure up to an external standard of laws and rituals. It is not something we do for Him. God continuously cleanses our hearts through His sanctification process so that we become more and more like His Son Jesus. Thus, the focus of God is not so much on judging our external actions and rituals but on changing our hearts.

6. **Which of the three alternatives is evident in the way you live, think, and feel? Journal how you feel about the way you experience Christianity.**

## Forsaking the Law Mindset

Most Christians I encounter live out of the second alternative. We were saved by Grace but now work to be kept by the Law. In Galatians 5, a group of Judaizers taught that Jesus-plus-circumcision was needed for salvation. Judaizers did not accept the true gospel and may have been spies sent by the Jews into the new Christian faith to stir up trouble. The real issue at hand was not circumcision. The real issue was that in order to become a Christian and go to heaven, they were adding something to Jesus' completed work on the cross. In this case it was Jesus-plus-circumcision. Paul exposes this falsehood.

*¹Behold, I, Paul, say to you that if you receive circumcision, Christ will be of no benefit to you. ²And I testify again to every man who receives circumcision that he is under obligation to keep the whole law. ³You have been severed from Christ,* **you who are seeking to be justified by law; you have fallen from grace.** *⁴For we, through the Spirit, by faith, are waiting for the hope of righteousness. ⁵For in Christ Jesus neither circumcision nor uncircumcision means anything, but faith working through love. (Galatians 5:1-5, emphasis mine)*

This was never how I understood the phrase "fallen from grace." Many of us grew up with this phrase used in the context of a believer who was doing fine in his/her walk with the Lord, but recently had done something pretty bad and was now labeled a person who had fallen from grace. This is how it might be said: "Old Joe hasn't been to church in months. I hear he is back on the sauce. He was such a fine Bible study teacher. He sure has fallen from grace."

Galatians 5:4 runs contrary to the way many interpret this phrase "fallen from grace." We make it out to be that the sin of a person has caused them to fall from God's grace; when in reality, it is those of us who put ourselves back under the Law who have fallen from grace. This is quite different from how the phrase has evolved into a toxic belief. It turns God's Word around and implies that if you don't measure up to the Law or the church's laws and expectations, you will fall from grace and from God's love, mercy, and forgiveness. You may even lose your salvation, according to this toxic lie.

Vines Expository Dictionary defines *severed* (from Christ) as "reduced to inactivity." (Remember, we cannot lose our salvation.) Also, the phrase *fallen from grace* (verse 4) means you are back to trusting rituals, good works, and your ability to perform to keep you in God's good graces.

"All of your righteousness [self-effort] is as filthy rags," says the Lord. (Isaiah 64:6) Jesus says: "For the sake of your tradition [the rules handed down by your forefathers] you have set aside the Word of God [depriving it of force and authority and making it of no effect]." (Matthew 15:6)

Unfortunately, over the centuries and even today, people believe in another gospel that is not the gospel: Jesus-plus-something-else will save us from His consuming fire and will keep us in God's good graces. Below you will find a very limited list of the lies allowing the law to creep back into Christianity.

- ☐ *Jesus plus* circumcision saves you.
- ☐ *Jesus plus* baptism as an infant saves you.
- ☐ *Jesus plus* total immersion as an adult saves you.
- ☐ *Jesus plus* belonging to a particular denomination saves you.
- ☐ *Jesus plus* worshipping on Saturday (Seventh Day Adventist) saves you.
- ☐ *Jesus plus* being on duty as a servant at all times saves you.
- ☐ *Jesus plus* daily Bible study and prayer saves you.
- ☐ *Jesus plus* not wearing pants, makeup, or jewelry saves you.
- ☐ *Jesus plus* not drinking, smoking or dancing saves you.
- ☐ *Jesus plus* centuries of traditions adhered to saves you.
- ☐ *Jesus plus* going to church every Sunday and on and on.

You may add your own *Jesus plus* ...

Cults have grown as so called "new revelations" were thought necessary in addition to the Word of God. A cult denies the true gospel of God, believing instead that their way of doing religion is the only way to God. *Jesus plus* what Ellen G. White added to the Bible (Seventh Day Adventist). *Jesus plus* what Joseph Smith added to the Bible (Mormonism). *Jesus plus* what Mary Baker Eddy added to the Bible (Christian Scientist). *Jesus plus* the Gnostic gospels (added some 200 years after the New Testament canon). *Jesus plus* traditions the Catholic Popes have added to the Word of God. Down through the centuries people tried to add to the Bible. These additions nullify the wonder and grace of God.

God's truth is found in *Alternative Three: Saved by Grace, Live by Grace.* "God is love" (1 John 4:8). God loves you in spite of your weaknesses, in spite of your sins. He loves you just because you are His child. He loved you so much that He sent His Son to pay the penalty for your sin. Because of Jesus, we are saved by grace. And we can only truly live by that grace.

Ever since I walked the isle to the front of my church and professed my faith in Christ, I wanted to be on God's team and validate His will for my life. But like Paul, this deep longing was not fulfilled, because I could not figure out how to live so I would be like Jesus. I believed I had to measure up to God's holy Law. But I couldn't do it! At the age of seventeen, I tried to set myself free of God. I didn't leave because I was angry with God. I left because I was angry with me. I could not do the things His Law required. I went off to make my way on my own. I had no idea how close I was to the kingdom of God when at age seventeen I had reached the end of myself and trying to be good on my own. (Recall the fourth purpose of the Law? *The Law Drives Us to God*) Believing I could not do the things His will demanded is the very place the Ministry of Condemnation wanted me to be. Unfortunately, I did not understand there was a Ministry of Acceptance. It was thirteen years before I discovered the Ministry of Acceptance. By God's grace when I was thirty,

I laid down my inabilities for God's ability in me. His grace is so precious to me that I wonder how many others have walked away, either physically, emotionally, or spiritually from the Ministry of Condemnation, mistakenly believing it is the gospel.

**7. Do you have a Law mindset? How do you know?**

**8. List any *Jesus plus* toxic beliefs you have lived under.**

# Paul's Journey to Freedom

Instead of accepting God's estimation of ourselves (sinners who can't measure up), most of us play games. We desperately try to cover up our blemishes and try to believe we can prove our value and worth. Remember, if you want to be accepted by God based on your own merits, the standard is perfection. When the emphasis is on you and your good actions, you are glorified. The emphasis is not on God and His efforts on our behalf.

This mindset is humanism, not Christianity. The true gospel comes by grace: we admit we are sinners who cannot measure up and thank God for sending Jesus to do for us what we could never do for ourselves. We cannot get to God on our own merits. We glorify God because the emphasis is on what God did for us, not the other way around.

Paul found this grace when he cried out in agony "Oh [unhappy and pitiable and] wretched man that I am! Who will release and deliver me from [the shackles of] this body of death?" (Romans 7:24) In joyous glee Paul thunders the answer, "Oh thank God [He will!] through Jesus Christ [the Anointed One] our Lord." (Verse 25) God's bright light of love came crashing in on Paul as the true gospel of Jesus Christ set him free of his inner conflict and guilt. He reviews his struggle by saying, "So then indeed I [of myself with the mind and heart] serve the Law of God but with the flesh, [I serve] the law of sin."

Does Paul's struggle remind us of our inner struggle, parts of ourselves warring within us? Paul said he was trapped in this cycle of trying but failing to measure up to God's Law. He realized that *God had set him free from trying to measure up because of the finished work of His Son, Jesus Christ who was perfect for us.* Romans 7 would not be complete without looking at Romans 8:1a: "Therefore, [there is] **now** no condemnation [no adjudging guilty of wrong] for those who are in Christ Jesus." Grace and acceptance came to Paul in Jesus. The war with himself and his war with God ended. In Christ, Paul is in full agreement with God. When he fails to measure up, he knows in his heart there is no more condemnation for failing! (Romans 8:1). The gospel set him free to step out in faith each day knowing in his heart, "I am loved by the God of this universe if I succeed or if I fail." This is freedom, my friend. Guilt, shame, and condemnation are removed. Paul is out from under the Ministry of Condemnation.

Do you see it? You who are in Christ are no longer judged guilty by God. Not because we are such good keepers of the Law. No! When we acknowledge we are inadequate to keep God's laws and accept the reality that Jesus took our sins away on the cross, God pronounces us *not guilty*. Jesus paid the penalty for us; we don't earn it with our own work. Praise God! As a Christian you are free of any condemnation from God ever again.

Jesus gives us entrance into God's forever family with the forgiveness of our sins. God took action on our behalf because we were caught in a dilemma: we are called to a perfection we cannot achieve, yet we are condemned for falling short of that perfection. God is the One who personally alleviates our dilemma because He loves us so much! "The wages of sin is death, BUT the free gift of God is eternal life in Christ Jesus our Lord." (Romans 6:23) The true gospel of Jesus Christ is simple and clear. "For by grace you have been saved through faith; and that not of yourselves, it is the gift of God; not as a result of works that none should boast." (Ephesians 2:8-9)

Salvation is an act of God on our behalf. If salvation came as a result of our good works, we could brag in our own ability to save ourselves. Many in the world believe, "God will accept me because I am a good person. I live a moral life." This is a Law mindset, which denies the truth that I cannot ever be good enough to be as perfect and holy as God. Goodness only comes as a result of our salvation. Jesus-plus-nothing, by grace and through faith, brings our gift of salvation.

Our striving to measure up flies in the face of God. Why? "If righteousness comes through the law, then Christ died needlessly." (Galatians 2:21b) When we are trying to obtain God's acceptance and favor or keep God's acceptance and favor by measuring up to a standard, or trying to be good, we are in effect saying, "Jesus, You died needlessly for me. It doesn't matter what You did for me. I will prove to You, myself, and others that I am worthy." If this is where you are in your thinking, then for you, Christ died needlessly. If Christ has set you free, then set yourself free from your own war with yourself.

9. **Even though you know you cannot keep the Law perfectly, do you expect yourself to do so? What do you really think about living in God's grace when you don't measure up?**

## In Summary

The Ministry of Condemnation insists we cannot keep God's Law, and prepares us to accept God's solution the

Ministry of Acceptance. These two ministries are uniquely different. When trying to mingle the two, we discover we have ruined both of them. When grace (the Ministry of Acceptance) is exchanged for the Law (the Ministry of Condemnation) we have sadly bought into another (false) gospel that will afflict and torment us.

The Law cannot make us right with God and He knows that. All the Law can do is declare a standard and condemn us for not keeping the standard. The purpose of the Law is to bring us to a place of desperation where we choose to receive or reject God's way of escape from His requirement of perfection. And that way is accepting the reality that Jesus took our sins on Himself and now desires to live His resurrected life in and through us.

Approaching God by the Law or by grace will have a far-reaching and very different impact on our lives and the lives of others. Our choice determines the quality of our spiritual and relational lives. Do you think you have to keep the Law? If you don't keep the Law, will God be angry with you or reject you? Or do you know God accepts you by grace just as you are, and so you love to serve Him? Do you love God's Law because under grace you understand God is committed to helping you mature? Our desire to obey the Law then comes out of gratitude and love for the One who lives in us.

Under the Law we walk in continuous condemnation. Under grace we can walk in freedom, peace, and rest. Wouldn't you like to be free of perfectionism, that unending struggle to measure up? We cannot measure up to society's standards or our own personal standards, much less God's standards. Perfectionism is a harsh taskmaster. Good enough is never good enough. We are saved by grace, through faith that is God's gift to us: it is simply Jesus-plus-nothing that saves us.

10. **Journal your thoughts about condemnation and grace. How does your condemnation of yourself impact your life?**

# CHAPTER 4

# GRACE: IT'S TRULY AMAZING

## *The Heart Of God Esteem*

### *Jesus as Lord*

*The Lord and I had walked along side by side for much too long. We continued on the journey together, my eyes fixed ahead, Bible tucked in my arms. Although comfortable with Him, a tension had been growing within me. I finally reached a peak of agony as I kicked through mounds of colorful leaves on our way along the path of life. The church bell rang out in rhythm with our steps as we approached the meticulously maintained church grounds. Our privacy soon to be interrupted, I could bear it no longer.*

*Reversing my direction, I stepped over directly in front of Him. Face-to-face now, His robe enveloped my frame in the breeze. I took hold of Him firmly by the shoulders as my Bible and sweater crunched into the leaves below. I swung stray hair from my face. Staring up at Him I cried, "I cannot stand this formality! I cannot stand just walking along beside You!"* I kicked off my heels, eyeing Him on my bare feet. *"Don't You understand? All this routine, churchy-churchy do another Bible lesson and sing another chorus and pray another prayer is no more than superficial fluff to me without a sensational relationship with You!"*

*Releasing my grip on Him I fell into His chest. Wrapping my arms around Him so tight, I heard Him exhale. "I delight in you!" He whispered. I gasped and squeezed Him even tighter, pressing my cheek into His shoulder. Hot tears poured from my eyes and bled into His robe. Without a word, He fixed His arms firmly around me. A smile of satisfaction eased onto my face as His embrace seeped through me in nourishment to my soul. It welcomed me home.*

*By Ashley Wille*

## The Heart of God Esteem

*Amazing grace—how sweet the sound—that saved a wretch like me! I once was lost but now am found, was blind but now I see. Twas grace that taught my heart to fear, and grace my fears relieved; how precious did that grace appear, the hour I first believed.*

What is the universal appeal of the hymn *Amazing Grace*, written by ex-slave trader John Newton, that Bill Moyers would host a four-hour secular television special featuring this one song? The song seems to be received by believers and non-believers alike. Are we not all singing about the Good News of the Gospel of Jesus Christ? The song speaks of our being wretches who are lost and blind; however, because of grace we are found, can see, and our fears are calmed. How curious that this remarkable song stirs the very people who reject the gospel of Jesus Christ. Could it be that the Spirit of God ministers, offering grace to the non-believer whenever *Amazing Grace* is sung? This is certainly our hope. In our last chapter, we considered the Ministry of Condemnation and its purpose. If this is the only reality a person knows, they often think they know what Christianity is. They need to be introduced to the Ministry of Acceptance, so they will understand the true gospel.

**1. What thoughts come to you as you think about Amazing Grace? Journal about how you feel.**

### *The Ministry of Acceptance*

The Ministry of Acceptance builds God Esteem. I pray as you read this chapter you will understand more of how loved you really are. Since you are so loved and so much is given to you, I hope you will treasure yourself and accept yourself as God already has. The Ministry of Acceptance is God's ministry of grace to us.

Many have tried to pen a meaningful definition of *grace*: one that captures the essence and depth of God's love. *Vines' Expository Dictionary of the New Testament* defines grace as *charis*: a sense of favor; to be in favor with God and Jesus Christ; unmerited favor and spiritual blessing from God to you. Applying a more practical definition, grace is about God in His love saving us from Himself (a consuming fire) and His wrath.

God offers His Son and we receive Him as our Lord and Savior. He offers us His grace and we receive it for ourselves. Many Christians have difficulty receiving God's grace, which includes all that He has prepared for us, not only for eternity, but for this present world. God's name is "I

AM." He is not "I was" or "I will be." I AM is present with you now, minute by minute.

**2. How do you know you are in favor with God? Journal how you feel about this.**

### *Acceptance and Grace*

The word *acceptance* gets closer to the true meaning and application of grace. Because the word *love* is so over-used and misused, acceptance seems even more personal than love. We may say we long for love but in reality we are longing for acceptance. We long to be known and accepted for the real person we are: the person behind the walls, the masks, and the games. Dr. Charles Solomon expresses this beautifully in his poem:

### A Fundamental Human Need

*Oh, to know acceptance*
*In a feeling sort of way;*
*To be known for who I am,*
*Not what I do or say.*
*It's nice to be loved for*
*The person I seem to be,*
*But my heart cries out to be loved,*
*For the person who is really me.*
*To be able to drop all the fronts,*
*And share with another my fears.*
*Would bring such relief to my soul,*
*Though accompanied with many tears.*
*The path to feeling acceptance of God*
*Is paved with acceptance on earth.*
*Being valued by others I love*
*Enhances my own feeling of worth.*

*Oh the release and freedom God gives*
*As I behold His wonderful face,*
*And Jesus makes real my acceptance in*
*Him, And I learn the true meaning of grace.*

*By C.R. Solomon*

You may have experienced more rejection than acceptance as a child, and even as an adult. But just one person in your life who accepts you can open your heart to see why acceptance is really healing. Being accepted for who we are, in spite of our mistakes, our sins, our behaviors or lack thereof, and even our failures, feels unnatural. Accepting God's acceptance is foreign to us. Jesus tells his followers, "I do not call you servants [slaves] any longer, for the servant does not know what the master is doing. But I have called you my friends, because I have made known to you everything that I have heard from my Father." (John 15:15) The fact that we can be called friends of God is truly perplexing, confounding, humbling, yet strangely soothing.

We can see the distinction between love and acceptance in the following dialog. In the book *Classic Christianity: Life Is Too Short to Miss the Real Thing!* the author asks his adult son:

*Father: Son, do you really know I love you?*
*Son: One thing I have always known is that you love me. I have never doubted your love, Dad.*
*Father: I really do love you, but let me ask you another question. Have you always known that I accepted you? That I accept you just like you are? That I really like you?*
*Son: There was a long pause in the conversation. Finally, the son looked up at his dad with tears in his eye and said. "No, Dad. I have never felt that you accepted*

*me. I feel I let you down many times, especially when
I chose not to go into the ministry."*

Acceptance is powerful in a person's life. I may know
that someone close to me loves me, that they have a deep,
abiding care for me. Yet I can also think this person does not
accept who I really am. All of us desperately want to belong,
to experience acceptance and validation as a person of incred-
ible worth. More often than we would like to admit, we are
more familiar with feelings of condemnation, rejection,
and separation. God's character of perfection and holiness
compels Him to love us with a higher standard of love than
any of us have ever experienced (*agape* love). Acceptance is
essential to the meaning of grace. Love divorced from acceptance becomes meaningless in our personal lives. Love and
acceptance go hand in hand. God accepts me not because of
my best but in spite of my worst. This is the heart of God
Esteem.

**3. Who has given you acceptance in your life? Journal
how this acceptance makes you feel. If no one has ever
accepted you for who you are, journal how this makes
you feel.**

### Debt or Grace

When people asked Jesus, "What are we to do, that we
may [habitually] work the works of God? [What are we to
do to carry out what God requires?]?" Jesus answered by
saying, "This is the work [service] God requires of you;
that you believe in the One whom He has sent [that you
cleave to, trust in, rely on and have faith in His messenger]."
(John 6:28-9) Surprisingly, our work is to believe in God's
ability working on our behalf. We are to do good for others;
however, our first work is from the inside out. Grace means

God does not need our ability in order for Him to be faithful to us. Grace is undeserved. There is nothing you can do, or not do, to receive God's grace. It is unconditional. In truth, grace is another way God shows us He loves us. We are officially His beloved children, by His grace, not because we have done anything for Him.

Some may argue, "We do owe God something, we owe Him our very lives and our obedience because of all He has done for us." We do praise Him for His grace, but owing something indicates a debt we must pay. A debtor is expected to pay something back to the lender. Grace has no debt connected with it.

Remember the parable of the king and the debtor. (Matthew 18:23-35) The debtor owed the king a huge sum of money yet the king forgave his debt. When you forgive someone's debt, they have indeed owed you something; it could be money, time, work, service, etc. Originally, an agreement was entered into between the king and the debtor. The debtor would pay back that which was agreed upon. Our king, however, forgave the man's debt. He now owed the king nothing. The king himself took the penalty of having no payment for the debt owed by the debtor.

God is just like this king, and we are the debtors. By God's decree, through the gift paid for by Jesus, we have been forgiven all the debt we owed God because of our sin. In place of our debt we have been given grace, unconditional, unmerited favor and spiritual blessings, the free gift of God. God only desires that anything we do, we do for Him because we love and appreciate Him. We serve Him because of our love for Him, not because we owe Him anything. His gift is free. God does not operate quid pro quo.

In our stead, Jesus walked in perfect harmony with His Father, living a perfect sinless life for us. He kept the letter of the law. Why did He do this? "But God commended his own love toward us, in that, while we were yet sinners, Christ

89

died for us." (Romans 5:8) He did it because He knew if He did not live out a perfect, godly life for us and then take our deserved punishment, there would be no hope of us ever being a part of the family of God. Someone on the radio recently said, "The God of this universe punished Himself so He might rescue us." How profoundly humbling and over-whelming is that? It is His good intent and His good pleasure to bless us.

"May blessings [praise, laudation, and eulogy] be to the God and Father of our Lord Jesus Christ [the Messiah] who has blessed us in Christ with every spiritual [given by the Holy Spirit] blessing in the heavenly realm!" (Ephesians 1:3) Think of the blessings God's grace provides us:

**Blessings of God's Grace**

☐ *He justified us (I am declared just, as if I had never sinned).*
☐ *He forgave us (past, present, and future).*
☐ *He gives us eternal security: even if you wallow in the mud of sin and are out of fellowship with God, God deems you are still a member of His family.*
☐ *Our guilt is lifted (There is therefore now no condem-nation for those who are in Christ Jesus).*
☐ *Righteousness (right standing with God).*
☐ *We receive the mercy of God, not the justice of God.*
*(See Supplemental Materials for more blessings)*

When you experience in your emotions the reality of grace, freedom comes that is challenging to explain. It is rest: freedom from your own efforts to make your relation-ship with God work. It is understanding: you know you are free and at one with God, just as you are. Jesus paid the debt of your sin. The war has ended between God and you. You are at peace with Him.

Brennan Manning writes in *The Ragamuffin Gospel* that the good news is we can stop lying to ourselves. "The sweet sound of *Amazing Grace* saves us from the necessity of self-deception. It keeps us from denying that even though Christ was victorious, our battle with lust, greed, and pride still rages within us. As a sinner who has been redeemed, I can acknowledge I am often unloving, irritable, angry, and resentful with those closest to me. When I go to church I can leave my white hat at home and admit I have failed. God not only loves me as I am, but also knows me as I am. Because of this I don't need to apply spiritual cosmetics to make myself presentable to Him. I can accept ownership of my poverty and powerlessness and neediness."

4. **Brennan Manning can go to church, leave his white hat at home, and admit he has failed. Why do you think that experiencing grace makes him able to do this? Can you do this?**

## Experiencing God

Does God want us to *experience* His grace? This is a question often tossed around in Christian circles; should we expect to experience God? Some say experience can be deceptive, and it can be. Looking at the Scripture, each one who ever truly represented God, experienced Him in their innermost being in a very personal way. Some even experienced a manifestation of Him in the physical realm; Moses at the burning bush was one such man. This is more than just mental assent given by saying "*I believe there is a God.*" There is a heart-felt experience of knowing God's love.

When we think in black and white we are moving into the law / legalism (dogma) at one end of a continuum. At the other end we can move into permissiveness. Dr.'s Cloud and Townsend encourage us to think in terms of "God's law balanced with God's grace balanced with time." We need time to grow deeper in our understanding of His love and will for our lives. This three-part balance allows us to step out in faith, trusting God's grace and trusting we will hear His voice. We know if we truly miss hearing Him, we are still "accepted in the beloved" (Ephesians 1:6). A passion for God coupled with trusting the grace of God means we win either way. We either hear Him rightly or we have an opportunity to grow in God's wisdom and truth when we do not hear Him rightly.

Experiencing God's love is His will for us, as we see in Paul's prayer for believers:

> *[16]May He grant you out of the rich treasury of His glory to be strengthened and reinforced with mighty power in the inner man by the [Holy] Spirit [Himself indwelling your innermost being and personality]. [17]And that Christ through our faith would dwell [settle down, abide make His permanent home] in our hearts! And that we would be rooted deep in love and founded securely on love. [18]And that we would have the power and be strong to apprehend and grasp with all the saints [God's devoted people, the experience of that love] which is the breadth and length and height and depth of it. [19]And that we would really come to know practically [through experience for ourselves] the love of Christ which far surpasses mere knowledge [without experience]; that we would be filled [through all our being] unto all the fullness of God [may have the richest measure of the divine Presence and become a body wholly filled and flooded with God Himself.] (Ephesians 3:16-19, emphasis mine)*

God desires for us to experience being strengthened and reinforced with mighty power in our inner being. He longs for us to experience His love and to know we are kept by His love. God wants us to apprehend and grasp with all the saints, those gone before us, and those still with us, the experience of His love. We are to be filled through all of our being with all the fullness of God. And we are to have the richest measure of the divine presence and be a body wholly filled and flooded with God Himself. We are to know all of this through personal experience in the love of Christ because experience far surpasses mere knowledge.

### 5. How have you personally experienced God? Journal your story.

#### *My Journey to Grace*

My journey to understanding God's grace and experiencing God's love may help you to see more of where you are in this journey. You might remember my story in an earlier chapter about the time I discovered how much I hated myself. After that visit with my therapist, I began the practice of going to my sofa and laying on it when I felt alone, helpless, and hopeless (depressed). I would purposely curl up, close my eyes and lie in the presence of God. I said nothing, thought nothing, envisioned nothing, and prayed nothing. I was prayed out, as they say. Strangely, I found this to be very soothing. I didn't know why. But I kept it up for several months.

So that you can understand where I was at this time, I must tell you a significant event that occurred when I was a young teen and had just broken up with the love of my life. My father, who was a kind and gentle man, came into my room. I was crying hysterically. He held me in his arms and lovingly said, "A coward dies a thousand deaths but a brave man dies but once." While it did not register until years later what this poem was personally saying to me, the emotional part of me immediately took in the meaning.

I had carried this unintended assault with me into adulthood. What did the poem say to me? It said I was a coward. This is an example of how lies come in and set up a stronghold in our hearts. I really do know that my father had no other intention but to love on me. Yet James tells us how dangerous our words are, regardless of how benign they may seem. As Christians we must remember there is another dimension to our world. Satan knows this is a danger to us. That day these words became a fiery dart that entered my soul and judged me a coward. From that day forward an internal dynamic that I did not know existed drove my life. We become what we believe. I believed, "I am a coward and I must cover this (so-called) truth at all costs."

6. **What do you really believe about who you are? Write out who you believe you really are. Remember don't just give a pat biblical answer. Answer what you really believe about yourself.**

### *Ending the War with Myself*

I didn't recognize the lie I was telling myself, but after fifteen years of being a Christian, the light of God's truth began to shine on this dark stronghold. There was a particular verse that seemed to minister to others that did not minister to me, I began to see a shadow of the lie. "Come boldly to my throne of grace and find help in time of need." (Hebrews 4:16) This simple direction was obvious. But it did not resonate in my heart of hearts as it seemed to do for others. Somehow, I believed I did not qualify. I was not bold. I was a coward. "How could I come boldly to God's throne room? I am a coward." Eventually, God exposed how I had wrongly focused on the word *boldly*. In my heart I had interpreted the meaning as, "I must go full of courage if I am going to go to the throne of grace or God won't be pleased."

One day as I lay on my couch in the presence of God, a picture of a rock fortress began to form in my mind. I began to flow along with this image. I was in this huge castle-like structure and all I could see were the large grey rocks of which the castle was built. I remember saying to God (not to Jesus, as Jesus was not in any way a part of this picture or in my mind), "Lord, can I put my little oval hooked rug down in this corner and just lie here in your presence. Lord, I have no more to give. I am tired. I am exhausted. I can't fix myself or the situation I find myself in. I give up. I am in despair. I just want to rest here in your presence."

I did not see God. I just sensed I was in His presence and I had His permission to just lie there in this weakened state. I lay on my small rug, thinking and picturing nothing else but what I have just described. A bit of time passed. I was soaking in being in the presence of God. Suddenly, from out of nowhere, Jesus walked toward me. He said nothing. I said nothing. But what He did in the next few moments released me from my self-hate and my works-of-righteousness attitude.

How do I explain? I will only fully understand what happened that day when I get to heaven. For the very first time, grace moved from my head into my heart and I really knew God loved me. Jesus walked over to me. I was on the floor in a fetal position on my little rug. He turned His back to the wall, slid down the wall, and sat on His haunches beside me. There were no words spoken between us but I could comprehend what He was saying. "I will sit with you for as long as you need me to as long as you are in this condition. It is OK to be who you are and where you are. You are welcome in my throne room in any state. You do not have to be anything for Me, except yourself in the moment." At this moment, the war with myself was over.

The impact of this experience was as momentous as the day when I asked Jesus into my life. The only way I can explain these two events is that when I was born again, my war with God ended. We made peace with one another. I realize now He was always willing to make peace with me but I was not willing to make peace with Him until one day in May of 1973 I took my stand with Him.

The war with myself had really ended! Because grace repels legalism, for the first time I knew deep in my being that I was accepted for *who I am,* not what I do. The Lord began to teach me how to treat myself with respect and take my own judgment off myself as He already had. I could be me and not be driven to measure up. And the amazing thing about not being driven is that you do not stay stuck in those things you don't like about yourself. These things begin to fade away. I do not understand this other than it being the grace of God working in me. This process continues even until today.

**7. Has the war with yourself ended? If not, what would your life be like if it did end?**

## In Summary

If we continue to allow the world system to have its way with us, lasting peace will elude us. Grace is God's Ministry of Acceptance. God showers His grace, mercy, and love upon us. Once we know experientially, deep within our hearts, the grace of God, we will revel in the glory and wonder of the love of God. Maybe for the first time in our lives, we feel loved and accepted. When grace becomes not just a theological idea, but an experiential reality, God's acceptance permeates every nook and cranny of our souls. We experience God on a deeper level than ever before. I find grace not only freeing but also addictive in a healthy sort of way. I know how much I need His grace! A continual fire in the belly burns brightly with the love and grace of God. My obedience now flows from a love relationship with God, not out of duty, debt or guilt.

## A Word of Caution

If you are anything like me, you will try to live under grace perfectly and then judge yourself for not doing *that* flawlessly. We are nothing but little dust people aren't we? However, "God is mindful that we are but dust" (Psalm 103:14) and loves us none the less!

# CHAPTER 5

# YOUR TRUE IDENTITY

## *Yours or Mine, God?*

### *Two Paths*

*I stand at a crossroads facing two paths. The wide path to my left winds around a steep rocky cliff covered with dark clouds and bolts of lightning. Legend has it that anyone who dares to reach the top of the mountain will be a god. Untold individuals have prided themselves on their strength and ability to brave its heights.*

*The narrow path straight ahead of me is barred by a constricted opening with hardly enough room to enter. Legend has it that anyone who passes through receives every perfect gift of heaven. Through the crack I can make out a path with many dangers, toils and snares... but the light beaming through the door seems inviting.*

*Which road shall I take? I am drawn to squeeze through the opening.*

*Bracing myself, I hold my breath and force through one body part at a time. Now through the*

*door a beautiful, beaming light invites me to follow.
Irresistible, it throws warm swirls around my heart
and fills my soul with joy. In the distance I can see
clearly the base of the mountain. Mounds of bones
speak for each and every climber who dared to
ascend.*

*By Ashley Wille*

In the Broadway musical *Jesus Christ Super Star*, there is a song with the lyrics, "Jesus Christ, Jesus Christ who do you say that you think you are?" As Christians we have a firm grasp as to who Jesus is. This question has already been settled for us. But what about, "Who do you say YOU think YOU are?" This is an age-old question, "Who am I?"

A child gets his identity from how he is treated by the adults in his family. He learns if he is loved, will be protected, and will be provided for. He discovers if he is emotionally and physically safe and whether he can trust or mistrust the people who care for him. What the child experiences determines his identity and what he thinks of himself.

We have no identity apart from our relationship with someone or something. We see ourselves in the mirror of someone else's eyes, and we believe what we see there. We may not like this identity, so we may latch onto practically anything in our desperate need for identity. People can determine their identities through their appearance, occupation, abilities, family relationships, intelligence, friends, denominational affiliation, influential people they know, and so on. The common denominator of all these human attempts to discover and to define our identity is they are all temporal. They can change within a twenty-four hour period of time and be gone.

As Christians we were (past tense) in the family of Adam, and our identity came from our family and the world system. Now we are in the family of God. Experiencing God Esteem is built upon our identity in Christ. The question at hand should be: Are we who *we* say we are, or are we who *God* says we are?

**1. What defines your identity? Journal your feelings about your identity.**

## Trapped

At 12 years old, as I mentioned earlier, I became trapped in an identity that would haunt me until I began to learn my true identity in Christ. In order to get my seventh grade teacher's favor, one had to be what she expected. I just didn't know how to be what she wanted me to be. I was a rather "chatty Cathy." To me, school was a social event. It was easy for me to step into her cross hairs. She was continuously on me about something.

One day after viewing an educational movie in the auditorium with my classmates, she asked me to stand. I had no idea what she was up to. She turned on the overhead projector and placed a picture of Venice de Milo on the screen. The real statue of Venice de Milo had lost her arms over the centuries. While I was standing, she remarked to the class, not to me, "If Micky keeps biting her fingernails like she does, she is going to look like this picture." She pointed to the picture of the statue. All the kids snickered. I was devastated, shamed, and humiliated in front of my peers. Yes, I should stop biting my nails. The teacher used humiliation to judge and condemn and hurt me in front of my classmates.

Did I stop biting my nails because of her humiliation? No, there was no motivation to do so. I just took on more pain of shame. What could she have done? She could have taken me aside during a bathroom break and said something like, "I think you are a cute girl, Micky, with a lot of friends, but I am concerned about your biting your nails. If there is anything I can do to help you stop, let me know and we can work on it together." This type of encouragement would have motivated me to stop biting my nails.

Numerous instances like the one just described happened over that seventh grade year. I believed something was wrong, really wrong, with me. Without understanding what was happening, I began siding with the teacher and took up the condemnation mantra against myself in my inner thought life. Emotionally, I agreed with what the teacher was pronouncing over me. I left myself and sided with her. I took on the identity reflected in how this teacher had treated me. Because of my own condemnation, shame followed me like Mary's little lamb. These internal condemnations produced bad fruit in my life. It influenced what I thought about myself and this influenced how I acted.

2. **Who reflected your identity to you as a child? How were you impacted by what they said?**

# Knowing Your History in Christ

I find many Christians accept Jesus as their Savior believe He died for their sins, took their sins on Himself, and will be with Him in eternity. They know Jesus suffered. They hear Him cry out, "It is finished!" They see Him die, taken down from the cross, put in the grave, and rise again. The end! They stand mystified at the empty grave, not understanding what relevance all this has for them in the here and now. Is this all there is to being a Christian: making sure our theology is correct and then defending that theology? Is Christianity just something to know about, to believe by faith and to experience at death?

Our wounded emotions are impacted positively when we understand who we are in Christ. Without our knowing and accepting who God says we are in Christ, we will struggle in our walk much like a person who has lost a leg and knows nothing of having a prosthetic. 2 Peter 1:4 tells us why He has given us these gifts: "God has granted (past tense) to us His precious and magnificent promises, in order that by them we might become partakers of the divine nature having escaped the corruption that is in the world." (Parentheses mine) God promises to move us toward partaking in God's divine nature in order to escape the corruption that is in this world.

Understanding Jesus' death, burial, and resurrection is more than mere academic knowledge that we affirm. Upon believing in Christ, something miraculous happens to us. No matter what the year, 1109 or 2009, when a person comes to Him in faith, within a nanosecond God does for us what we could never do for ourselves. In just three days God completed the grand plan, which He foresaw before the foundation of the world. Before time began, He set into motion what He continues to do for every person who comes to Him in faith.

Throughout the New Testament, especially in the Epistles, there are many verses telling us how much God has done (past tense) for us to make us acceptable to Him. God lives outside of time. Time began when He created the world and time will end when Jesus returns. Because God does not operate in time, He takes each of us at the moment we pray to receive His Son, back 2000 years to the cross and puts us in Christ as Jesus is being crucified. We see this in Romans 6:3-5:

> *3Are you ignorant of the fact that all of us who **have been** baptized into Christ Jesus **have also been** baptized into His death? 4We **were buried** with Him by the baptism into death, so that just as Christ **was raised** from the dead by the glorious power of the*

*Father, so that we too might habitually live and behave in newness of life. ⁵For if we **have become** one with Him by sharing a death like His, we shall also be one with Him in sharing His resurrection. (**emphasis** mine)*

"Are you ignorant?!!" is usually stated as a rhetorical question. However, it seems most Christians could answer, "Yes, I am ignorant of all God has done for me." Look back at the words *have been*, *were*, *was*. According to the past tense in this passage, note what was done for you and me: *finished* and *completed* 2,000 years ago.

We were in Christ when Christ died. When He died, we died with Him. When Jesus was buried, we were buried with Him. And, when Jesus was raised from the dead, we too were raised from the dead with Him. Why? It is only after we die in Christ and are raised to a new life that we can live and behave in newness of life. The old self is dead. This is a radical transformation.

On the day of the resurrection, Jesus is called the first-born of the Father (Romans 8:29). Since Jesus is the first-born, there was a second-born and then a third-born and so on right down to us. God is our Father and Jesus is our elder brother. We were taken out of the kingdom of darkness and translated into the kingdom of light! (Colossians 1:13) We are God's children, just as Jesus is.

Where might you have been the forty days after Jesus' resurrection? *In Christ* is the correct answer. You were also in Christ when Jesus rose into the heavens. Where might you be today? Ephesians 2:6 says, "And He [God] raised us up together with Christ and made us sit down together [giving us joint seating with Him] in the heavenly sphere by virtue of our being in Christ [Jesus the Messiah, the Anointed One]." We have joint seating with Christ today!

His prayer to His Father was answered, "…that they (*you and me*) all may be one, [just] as You, Father, are in Me and I in You, that they (*you and me*) also may be one in Us, so that the world may believe and be convinced that You have sent Me." (John 17:21, *parentheses mine*) The Holy Spirit is in us. You and I are in Christ. Christ and you and I are in God!!! We are completely covered inside and outside!

**3. Using the analogy above from John 17:21, journal how you feel about these questions: Where are you? Where is Christ? Where is God?**

### *Christ is in Me*

I was ignorant of this history in Christ, even though I was raised in a church that had altar calls each Sunday, giving people the opportunity to ask Jesus into their lives. I could not comprehend what it meant to accept Jesus into my life. Every Sunday the pastor said, "If anyone would like to receive Jesus Christ as their personal Lord and Savior come to the front of the church and make a public confession." I sat mystified.

I did not understand what it meant to *be* a Christian, much less *how* to be a Christian. Years later, a friend invited me to a prayer breakfast. I was not sure what this meant, but I accepted the invitation purely because I wanted to see and be seen at the lovely country club where the event would be held, and would be hosted by a volunteer organization I desired to join. I am sure God planned it this way! He knew He would not catch me in a church. I was, however, in my element and felt emotionally safe at the club.

You wouldn't have seen it, but inside, I was really struggling. At thirty years old, I suddenly was bored with my tedious life. All the glitter of life had let me down. I had all I needed of it to see it would take me nowhere; at least nowhere I wanted to go. Climbing the social ladder would not give me an identity I would be honored to have. I was tired of the struggle within between God and myself: would I give my life to Him or not? I was sick and tired of having no real sense of self, of living the life of a chameleon with no purpose in life.

The speaker began to talk about her life and a theme very familiar to me. She set her mind to get something, but when she acquired it, her enthusiasm for it burst like a bubble. When she got what she wanted, it gave her no satisfaction. I was much too familiar with this theme, and I sensed a strong emotion of sadness as I was drawn into the speaker's story.

At the end of her talk she said, "If you would like to invite Jesus into your life…" "Oh, not again!" I moaned to myself. "I just don't get it." She went on to say the words that ushered me out of the kingdom of darkness into the kingdom of light. She continued, "Invite Jesus into your life and let Him use your hands, your feet, and your mouth to walk around the streets of Atlanta sharing God's love." Zap! I got it!

I remember exactly what was going through my mind. "Do you mean there is someone who will live the Christian life for me and that someone is Jesus? This is how you live the Christian life? Wow!" I prayed to receive Christ. Remember, God was meeting me at my most vulnerable place: I needed someone to take care of me. He meets us at our place of need. Each conversion is uniquely personal.

I invited Christ into my life, therefore Christ was in me. As Galatians 2:20 states, "I have been crucified with Christ; and it is no longer I that live, but Christ living in me: and that life which I now live in the flesh I live in faith, the faith which is in the Son of God, who loved me, and gave himself up for me." He was going to do the work in and through me. It was not about my trying to do what Jesus would do. A magnificent fire of hope and love began to burn in my heart, a love that has burned brightly for thirty-three years. I was finally in the family of God. My war with God had ended.

What else happens to us at the hour we first believe? We instantly are given the Holy Spirit. The Holy Spirit comes into our dead spirits and makes us alive. We are born into God's Family. This is where the phrase *born again* comes from. "You have been regenerated [born again], not from a mortal origin [seed, sperm], but from one that is immortal by the ever living and lasting Word of God." (1 Peter 1:23) We were once born of human sperm; now we are born of the spirit: born a second time.

When I was born again I had no words to express what happened to me. All I knew was something unbelievably wonderful had happened. I was filled with joy and excitement about God. I wanted to know everything I could about Him and how to let Christ live His resurrected life in me. Several weeks after my big moment with God, I was telling a Christian friend what happened to me. Upon finishing she said, "You were born again." I said, "What?" She explained in detail the meaning of this phrase. I was no longer ignorant and had words to express my experience. I was born again!

At the moment we are born again we are sealed with the Holy Spirit. "In Him, we also, after listening to the message of truth, the gospel of our salvation having also believed, we were sealed in Him [Christ] with the Holy Spirit of promise, who is given as a pledge of our inheritance, with a view to the redemption of God's own possession, to the praise of His glory." (2 Corinthians 1:22, New American Standard version) Like a child whose hand is stamped as he pays for his ticket to the carnival, we too are stamped. The child can freely go out and come back through the gate because he has the official carnival stamp that indicates he paid for his ticket.

Jesus paid for our ticket on the cross. That payment gets us through the gate and into the Father's throne room during our life here on earth and later into heaven when we die. The child's stamp will wash off, but the Holy Spirit's stamp is permanent and can never be removed. It lasts an eternity.

Other things happen at the same time. God could not seal you with His Holy Spirit until your temple has been cleansed, so He cleanses our temples for us. 2 Corinthians 5:21 tells us, "God made Jesus [who did measure up to God's perfection] who knew no sin, to become sin on our behalf [who would never be able to measure up and would always be inadequate in ourselves] so that we might become the righteousness of God in Christ Jesus." (Brackets mine). This is called *The Great Exchange*.

What a transaction! Jesus takes our sins on Himself and we get His righteousness. Because of Jesus' work, we now measure up just like Jesus measures up, but not because of anything we do. Our acceptance is based on what God the Father did through His Son for us.

**4. Journal how your war with God ended—or has it? What new truths have you gleaned in this section about what God has done for you?**

### *I Am In Christ*

I had finally accepted Jesus as my Savior, and I knew that Christ was in me. But I had so much more to learn and experience! At thirty-eight I attended a Bible study focused on understanding that our identity is to come from God alone. I learned that I am not who the world system tells me I am. I was fascinated and encouraged as my teacher challenged us to read the Epistles and circle every occurrence of *in Christ, by Christ*, and *through Christ*. Eager to discover my true identity, I decided to find and write out all of the verses I could find. As the list became longer and longer, I was overwhelmed by God's estimation of me and all that He had done for me. I began to understand the good news of the gospel: everything I need is found in Christ!

More than 140 passages use the similar phrases *in Christ, in Him, in Whom,* and *through Him.* For every verse that tells us Christ is in us, there are ten verses that say we are in Christ. Some examples:

*Ephesians 1:7—In Him we have (present tense) redemption [deliverance and salvation] through His blood, the remission [forgiveness] of our offences, in accordance with the riches and the generosity of His gracious favor.*

*Romans 8:1—There is therefore now (present tense) no condemnation for those who are in Christ Jesus.*

*I Corinthians 1:2—To the church of God which is at Corinth, to those who have been (past tense) sanctified in Christ, saints by calling with all who in every place call upon the name of our Lord Jesus Christ, their Lord and ours.*

*2 Peter 1:3—God has given (past tense) us everything pertaining to life and godliness through the true knowledge of Jesus who called us. (Parentheses mine)*

*(See Supplemental Materials for more Identity Verses)*

These verses are only samples of the 140 other benefits we have already been given. The day before you received Jesus' blood-bought gift you may have told yourself, "I can't measure up. I will never be holy." You are right. You cannot measure up to God's standard and you can never make yourself holy in and of yourself, but God can and has.

These verses say you have salvation and forgiveness of sins. It is a gift. This is grace! And God will never ever condemn you. God has already given us (past tense) everything that pertains to our being Godly and everything (present tense) that pertains to life. You are sanctified in Christ, a saint.

## 5. Journal about what it means for you to be in Christ.

### *Intimacy with God*

God first created us to enjoy fellowship, connection, and relationship with Him. When we accept Jesus for who He is and we are born into God's family, He considers us His children just as He does His Son Jesus. What a position of honor God has given us in Christ!

As His children we call Him *Abba*. "For ye received not the spirit of bondage again unto fear; but ye received the Spirit of adoption [the Holy Spirit] whereby we cry, Abba, Father. The Spirit himself beareth witness with our spirit, that we are children of God: and if children, then heirs; heirs of God, and joint-heirs with Christ." (Romans 8:15-17) The word *Abba* suggests familial intimacy. In English it means *papa* or *daddy*. This was unheard of and a stumbling block to the Jews, this kind of intimacy with God. They did not, and some still do not, write out the word God as we do. They would have written G_ _. No other religion purports such an intimacy with their God! The verse goes on to validate that we are not only children of God but joint-heirs with Christ. Everything that Jesus inherited from His Father now belongs to us also. We are not part of the Trinity, but God provided a way for each of us to have a connected, intimate relationship with Him just as Jesus has a connected, intimate relationship with Him.

In the context of this new self in Christ we understand how the Bible speaks to us about loving ourselves. We are in Christ. God's relationship with Jesus is one of love and acceptance, so we understand that God loves us at the same time Jesus is being loved by the Father, as we are in Jesus. As God accepts Jesus, God accepts us. Just as Jesus receives that acceptance, we too are to receive God's acceptance and take it as our own.

**6. Can you call God your daddy, your Abba? Journal your feelings about God as Abba.**

## Unshakable Identity

There is stability in having an identity that cannot be taken away from us. One foundational truth that cannot be shaken is, "I am a child of God." We might be a child of God who happens to be a business person, or a mother, athlete or the President of the United States; but our true identity comes from our Father. Only when our identity is based on who God says we are can we ever begin to discover emotional security.

The tragedy of many modern-day Christians is ignorance of who they are in Christ. After Jesus Christ did everything necessary to make us acceptable to a holy God and gave us His very life to experience every day, too many of us still thrash around in doubt as to whether God will really hear our prayers, whether we are worthy to be used by God or whether God really even cares about us. Esteeming ourselves as God does means discovering and accepting who God says we are. We must know who we are, not based on our genealogical history, but based on our spiritual history in Christ.

As I was teaching a Bible study on the Gospel of John, I became acutely aware of John referring to himself as "the disciple Jesus loves." The Holy Spirit quickened me: if John, a disciple of Jesus Christ, called himself this, and I am a disciple of Christ, why can't I say this about myself? With much humility and meekness I spoke out loud, "I am Micky Land, the disciple whom Jesus loves." It was grueling for me to get these words out. I said it again and again and again. The words began to sink into my soul. A sense of being loved by the God of this universe caressed me. I was beginning to experience my identity in Christ.

7. **Join me by saying aloud, "I am (insert your name) the disciple whom Jesus loves." Journal how you feel about saying this out loud?**

## Chosen Identity

At the beginning of this chapter you were asked, "Where does your identity come from? Are you who you have been telling yourself or are you who God says you are?" In order to collect an earthly inheritance we must willingly go to a lawyer's office and take it as our own. The same is true regarding your new inheritance in Christ. Your inheritance already exists. We just need to take it as our own. I've discovered God's process for *becoming* is always the same. I wanted Jesus in my life so I *took* Him into my life. If I need forgiveness then upon confessing I am to *take* His forgiveness. If I need to know I am accepted in Christ, then I am to *take* that acceptance and so on. I purposely use the word *take*. *Receive* is passive. *Take* is active. We are to *take* what God has provided for us.

God's actions on our behalf glorify Him because the emphasis is on what God does and commits to do for you and me. God is similar to a human father who is pleased to do something special for his child, and have the child take it. How would a father feel if the child refused to take his gifts? When we take God's gifts, we can know acceptance in spite of our sins and imperfections and rest in that reality. God's gift to us is Jesus' completed work on the cross. Our gift to

God is to take as our own all He gives us in Christ. Will you take God's family identity or will you keep your own?

8. **Have you chosen to take your identity from God, or from someone or something else? Journal your reality about this.**

## In Summary

God's performance on our behalf saves and keeps us, not our performance for Him. God's grace gives us a new identity we can never lose. Grace is practical because it defines who we are. We are loving ourselves when we agree with God as to who He says we are. We come to understand how God Esteem shapes our identity. No one can take away this identity, no matter how bad our circumstances. When our thinking changes, our emotions change and when our emotions change, then our actions change. This makes for a radical transformation.

The statement below is a partial description of your inheritance in Christ. Each element is based on Scripture.

**Spend a few moments reading this statement to yourself, about who you are in Christ. Afterwards journal which ones you feel very comfortable with. Which ones feel uncomfortable?**

*I am (your name), a child of God, a joint heir with Jesus Christ. I am accepted in the beloved and I am a beloved disciple of Jesus Christ. Jesus loves me! My love relationship with Jesus is not based on works, but on the free gift of God's grace. I am loved in spite of who I know I am. God is not surprised I am a sinner. He knows I am but dust, and loves me anyway. God loved me so much that He willingly sent His beloved Son, Jesus, to come to earth, to live as a man, and to die to pay for my sin. This is how much He loves me! When Jesus rose from the dead, He became living proof that He could give me a new life, too. His life is strong, but I am weak. He wants to be strong in me, so that He can use me to attract others to Him. He can use me because I know and acknowledge I am weak. It is in this weakness that He is strong on my behalf. God also can use my inadequacies, because He uses the foolish things of this world to confound the wise: He shows how strong He is by being strong in weak me. I may be weak on my own, but I am safely kept in Him. I am sealed for an eternity by the Holy Spirit. No one or no thing or action of mine can snatch me out of my Father's hands. Jesus will never leave me nor forsake me. God can take what is meant for evil toward me or by me and turn it into good. I never have to be afraid of my Father because He is ultimate mercy: He loves me and gives me the good I don't deserve. Because of Jesus' finished work on the cross, my Father works in my soul to grow me more and more into the image of Jesus. God created me for a purpose and He leads me into all He intended for me. One day, He promises, I will be perfect: complete, and whole, and strong, just like Jesus! (See appendix for verses.)*

# CHAPTER 6

# LOVING YOURSELF WITH BOUNDARIES:

## *Or Hurting Yourself by Codependency*

### *Boundaries*

*I have a sign on my front door. It says,* No Trespassing. *That lets people know they cannot barge into my house. They must knock and wait for me to open the door. If they do barge in, I tell them to leave and not to do it again. If they do, they will not be allowed in at all. In my house I make the rules and when people come into my house they must abide by them.*

*Sometimes people try to tell me my rules are bad. If I believe them, I will let them barge in every day. I used to do this and it would make me feel sad and angry because my house didn't feel like mine anymore. They started to think it was their house and would boss me around and not leave. Now I know my rules are good. They keep me safe and healthy.*

*Other people have rules, too. And I must abide by their rules if I want to be their friend. Sometimes I don't like their rules, but I must respect them if I want to keep my friends. One day my friend got mad at me because I snuck into her house to give her a surprise birthday cake. She does not like surprises at all. So, I will have to surprise her in another way if I want to keep her as a friend. Another time my friend told me he liked my hair and touched it. I told him if he ever did that again we would not be friends. So he agreed to respect my wishes.*

*One way I know my rules are being broken is that I feel bad inside. I must remember to think about why I feel bad and then address the issue. It's usually about my rules.*

*By Ashley Wille*

When the topic of Christian self-sacrifice is discussed in religious circles, along with healing from code-pendency, concern often arises that to be healed from code-pendency one must disregard significant biblical teachings. Codependency and Christian self-sacrifice are often viewed as being one and the same. When observed by others they look very much alike; however, they are quite different. Time, energy, and/ or money are poured into others by both. Christian self-sacrifice includes personal boundaries, whereas codependency does not. Codependency has hidden agendas, whereas Christian self-sacrifice does not. Boundaries help us break codependent behaviors in our lives.

Misinformation about the Bible's directives concerning the issue of setting boundaries with people has led to some confusion in the church. How can we be sure God wants us to have boundaries? One answer is because God has bound-aries and we can take our lead from Him.

## God's Boundaries

In their book *Boundaries,* Drs. Cloud and Townsend state "The concept of boundaries comes from the very nature of God. God defines Himself as a distinct, separate being Who is responsible for Himself. He defines and takes responsibility for His personality by telling us what He thinks, feels, plans, allows, will not allow, likes and dislikes. He also defines Himself as separate from His creation and from us. He differentiates Himself from others. He tells us who He is and who He is not."

According to God's example, a healthy, balanced Christian takes responsibility for his or her own God-given, unique personhood. This is exhibited when we step up and speak out: about what we think, what we feel, what specific plans God has given us, what we will allow into our lives, what we will not allow into our lives, what we like, and what we do not like. We are to take responsibility for being endowed by God with specific gifts and a specific mission that is distinct from all other Christians.

Seeing God's example, we are also to be emotionally separate individuals from the significant people in our lives. We are to be interdependent, not independent, and not codependent. Codependents become enmeshed (entangled) with a person or certain people in their lives; usually a spouse, a child, or sometimes a friend. *Enmeshment* is being exceedingly connected to another person so that the individual's emotions are dependent on the other person's emotions. If the other person feels great, the codependent individual feels great. If the other person is down, the codependent individual is down. If the other person does not do what is thought to be correct, a codependent individual projects what will happen to the other person and feels the pain that they believe the other feels (which may or may not be the case). A codependent individual needs to be needed, and feels the other person cannot handle things alone. The individual has a vested interest in getting the other person fixed. If the other person gets in some sort of trouble, the codependent will try to cover up the other person's actions and make excuses for them. They desire to fix them and to protect them.

Simply put, a codependent person feels overly responsible for another person, and cannot allow that person to fail. In this type of relationship, neither knows where one begins and the other ends. They keep each other emotionally sick until one of them breaks the cycle.

When we look to God as our example, we notice one of His boundaries is that He does not have a committed relationship with unrepentant sinners. God desires to have a relationship with everyone. By His grace, He invites everyone to repent and to enjoy a loving relationship with Him. But unrepentant sinners do not accept His grace, so in truth they do not really want to have a relationship with God. Because God is a consuming fire, requiring perfect holiness in His presence, His boundaries actually protect the unbeliever from instant annihilation. He sets a boundary by telling us in the Bible that He has made a way for us to be in relationship with Him and the way to Him is through His Son, Jesus. It is the only way to Him.

The Ten Commandments are an example of God's boundaries for us. The word *boundaries* could be exchanged for the words *rules, laws, limits, principles,* or *restrictions.* God knows what keeps us free from pain, distress, guilt, emotional, physical and spiritual upheaval in our lives. He created us to be in a loving relationship with Him, and he gave the Ten Commandments to show us how we were created to live. He warns us as a loving Father that if we stay within these boundaries we will remain free of the consequences of enslavement to things that will tear us apart.

Stepping over God's boundaries exposes us to strong outside forces that strike hard at our sin natures and our wills.

Outside God's protective boundaries, we can be swept away by forces that feel as strong as the ocean tide's undertow. We can find ourselves in places and circumstances where we never thought we would go. The eventual result is spiritual, emotional, relational, mental, and even physical pandemonium in our lives.

God's boundaries are easier to understand when we think of parents rearing a small child. The parents set boundaries for the child, for the sheer protection of that child. Boundaries include appropriate consequences attached to breaking or staying within the boundary. When the child breaks the parents' boundaries, the child is accountable to the parents for breaking the boundary. The child will then receive the consequence appropriate to breaking the boundary applied to him. The pain of the consequence shows the child the significance of breaking the parents' boundaries of protection. In a similar way, if we break God's boundaries, we are asking for painful consequences; if we don't want these consequences, we must stay within God's boundaries.

God has set immutable and absolute boundaries within the universe. God's boundaries always protect us, and breaking those boundaries will certainly work against us. He has given us the freedom to choose. Just as gravity certainly works when an object falls to the ground, God's boundaries also certainly work. Can we jump from the top of a building and expect any other result than the force of gravity taking over and pulling us toward the earth? If we jump, can we say that God maimed us? No. Our jumping (stepping over the boundary of gravity) and slamming into the ground maimed us. Neither God nor His boundary maimed us. We chose to jump. We maimed ourselves.

1. **As you think about God's boundaries, such as the Ten Commandments, how do His boundaries affect how you think, feel, and act?**

## Healthy Boundaries or Walls

Understanding how healthy boundaries are very different from walls allows us to respect the boundaries set by others and to set healthy boundaries for ourselves. Most of our major conflicts in relationships come from crossing other people's boundaries or allowing others to invade our personal boundaries. When we are confident about our boundaries - what we will allow and what we will not allow - healthy people will respect us and our boundaries. Boundaries are not walls. Walls encase and surround us, keeping us cut off from emotional intimacy. Walls keep us from our own self-awareness, leaving us with little or no understanding of how our actions and words impact others adversely. One friend described her walls to me, saying she feels like she's living in total darkness in a large silo used for storing wheat on a farm. What a horrible way to live, walled off from the beauty of intimate friendships and from life itself!

Some people have no boundaries. They allow anyone into their lives, resulting in relationships that are not emotionally safe. We each need safe, confidential people to share with, but the person with no boundaries will verbalize inappropriate information about themselves to anyone. Often this information is used by the other person to manipulate them. They are run over in these unhealthy relationships as if by a stampede of horses. The person with no boundaries has no way to stop the stampede.

Many of us get caught up in a seemingly endless helping mode that has no boundaries, creating a codependent relationship. The over-helper becomes burned out and resentful. The exhaustion sets off various scenarios that severely sabotage significant relationships. On the other hand, the over-helped never assumes personal responsibility for life issues. If this over-helped person ever realizes how this unhealthy protection has stunted their emotional growth and life, they will feel anger and resentment toward the over-helper.

The over-helper is often a parent who remains overly involved with a child. When the child becomes an adult, this adult will choose one of two paths. One path is to rebel and partially or completely divorce the parent. The parent will have no idea why the child has distanced himself unless the adult child explains, and the parent listens. With God's help the parent can allow the adult child to make his or her own way in life. The other direction is to continue to live with or supported by the parents for the rest of their lives. Neither is fulfilling; both are stifling. God is not glorified when a person's emotional growth is stifled, because He made us to be responsible to Him for our individual selves.

**2. Journal whether you have healthy boundaries, or walls, or no boundaries in your life. What might be the results of your having walls or no boundaries?**

### *Recognize Codependency*

One of the difficulties in creating healthy boundaries is that codependents most often are not aware of their true motives in helping others. Carol Smith, MS, MA, LPC, in the article *Codependency and Christianity* states: "Molding myself into what another needed had not turned out to be Good News. At the root, I was not laying down my life for others; I was laying down my life for myself—so others would stick around and, by needing me thus keeping me from sinking into my own pain. Somehow, I had come to identify this way of running from myself as being Christian."

## Some Characteristics of a Christian Codependent Helping Others

Makes decisions based on fear of rejection and the need to be accepted

Makes decisions based on not allowing others to be hurt

Believes in total self-sacrifice, leaving oneself out of their own network of care

Bases personal worth on an ability to care for and fix others

Has difficulty speaking up for themselves as to what they need or want to have happen in their lives

Compromises and accommodates to excess

Restricts open and honest expression of feelings and ideas

Has great difficulty acknowledging and meeting their own needs and desires

Has difficulty in knowing who they are as separate from the help they give

Feels loved and accepted by trying to live up to the Law (or being good by their chosen definition)

Is continually plagued by guilt that they are never helping enough

Continually struggles with experiencing God Esteem (which is appropriate self esteem)

Two important perspectives are missing from these codependent actions and feelings. First, the person looks to others for filling the leaking bucket of self esteem, rather than finding true God Esteem to plug the holes in that bucket: we must depend on God and His grace. Second, the person may not understand and has not truly accepted God's grace for daily living. God can lead us to be interdependent with others and work together to please God and to live within His boundaries.

**3. Are you aware of a codependent relationship in your life? Are you codependent with someone or is someone codependent with you? Journal your experience of this relationship.**

## *Guard Your Heart*

Walls divide us from others, and codependency enmeshes us with others, but healthy personal boundaries are permeable. Each of us is the gatekeeper to our own soul and body. We open the gate to let healthy people and healthy situations in and we close the gate to keep unhealthy people or situations out of our lives. We learn to make decisions about who is and is not safe and when to say *yes* and when to say *no*. This is how you learn to guard your heart.

Proverbs 4:23 states: "Guard your heart with all diligence, for from it flow the springs of life." Boundaries guard our hearts and souls. People who guard their hearts have external boundaries as well as internal boundaries. External boundaries allow us to choose our distance from other people and enable us to give or refuse permission for them to be our friends or to touch us. Internal boundaries protect our thinking, feelings, beliefs, choices, talents, values, desires, and behaviors. An internal boundary may need to be set at the end of a stressful day. In setting an internal boundary, we decide what we will bring into our hearts, and what we will not allow into our hearts. This healthy protection can prevent unhealthy self-soothing that many seek from overindulgence in excesses or addictive behaviors such as eating too many sweets, drinking too much alcohol, or looking at pornography.

Some of us who are too hard on ourselves have not yet set healthy internal boundaries. Healthy boundaries may say, "I am not judging myself today. If I do, I will suffer the consequences of a free fall into emotional instability, be that depression or anxiety. I will have upset my day – and for what?" We may believe that we should not have or express our needs or wants. Denying our needs and wants builds resentment against another person. Resentment builds to an outward explosion or an interior, private implosion that is emotional, physical, and/or spiritual. We burn out. When we do not set appropriate boundaries with others we are unwittingly choosing against ourselves. We can become prey for others to use us. If we continue without boundaries, being controlled by others can become a way of life for us.

A tragic news story illustrates how a lack of boundaries and denial leads to resentment and then to explosion. A young mother of three and wife of a pastor of a small church did not know to set boundaries with her husband. For years he privately forced her to dress as a prostitute and do things against her desire or will. One day, her internal rage exploded into external rage: she shot and killed her husband. By not setting healthy boundaries for herself, she had enabled him to continue to abuse her year after year. Without understanding what she was doing, she allowed evil in her life and home. Becoming an abused woman, she was teaching their girls to accept abuse from men. Her husband was also teaching their boys how to mistreat women. Please do not hear me laying blame on the wife. Was either the wife or her husband in the will of God? I think not. Sadly, because she was a pastor's wife she probably believed she had to keep her husband's actions secret to protect his ministry. She denied her own needs and wants for a healthy relationship; her resentment and the pain of abuse grew; and she lost hope that anything would change. She resorted to the unhealthy boundary at the end of a gun when she was at the end of herself. If we could ask her, I believe she would tell us that she never intended for any of this to happen. Healthy boundaries do protect us and others.

True faith and healthy boundaries work together to protect us. We do not have to renounce our faith in order to set boundaries. "Knowing what we are to own and take responsibility for gives us freedom. God designed a world where we inhabit our own souls and we are responsible for the things that make us up." (Cloud and Townsend) We must guard the precious, tender, and loving life in our souls. At the same time, we must let God help us determine those things in our souls that can be let go: things that hurt us and hurt others.

**4. What do you know you are to own and take responsibility for in your life now? Do you guard your heart? Journal a recent example of how you do this or how you wish you had done this.**

### *Include Yourself*

One way to guard my heart is to care for the person who is *me*. We easily care for others, but healthy boundaries show that I must be willing to include myself in my network of care. Codependents leave themselves out. God calls us to love our spouse, our children, our friends, strangers, our neighbors, and even our enemies. And, as we saw in Chapter Two, we are to also love ourselves. When I add myself into my network of care, I am loving myself in a healthy manner. I can set boundaries for myself and others. I begin to create a more balanced way to live.

I understand if I do not set boundaries, I am enabling irre-sponsibility. I become a partner with the other person helping them remain irresponsible. Boundary setting gives the other person the choice to take responsibility for him or herself. At one time or another each of us has dealt with a needy friend, a spirited and strong-willed child, a mother or mother-in-law who wants to control and manipulate us to do their will, a boss or husband who is either needy or controlling.

A common example may be seen when your cousin asks to borrow a sum of money. He promises to pay you back. In fact he has not paid back the first loan that you have already given him, but since you are a giving Christian you give him more money. Time passes and you ask for the money back. Your cousin says, "Sure, I'll get it to you." More time passes and you hear from your aunt that your cousin is in dire financial distress again. You figure you will not be getting your money any time soon. One evening the phone rings. It is your cousin. He is desperate. He tells you he was in an automobile accident and has no way to get to work. If he can't work, he can't pay his rent. You stop and think, "If I give him the money to fix his car, this money lending will go on forever. Plus, I need the money myself right now. I have not taken a vacation in five years and I am in the process of booking my reservations. But if I don't give him the money, he will go into a rage and blame me for ruining his life. And furthermore, he will mock my Christian faith. Using my money for a vacation right now is surely not Christian. Is it?"

You are between a rock and a hard place. Do you choose yourself to be the victim, giving him the money because you feel you have no other choice, or you need to take care of his situation to show you are a good Christian? Do you choose to take care of yourself and let him be the one who gets in a bind without a way to get to work? Could you, by not giving him the money, actually be helping him hit bottom so he will get help to make the changes he really needs to make? None of these answers would be completely satisfactory. These real-life questions show the struggle we often face when we don't set appropriate boundaries.

Boundaries are not an offensive weapon but a defensive weapon. They are set to protect us from hurt by others. We need to know how to discern between two different types of hurts. One type of hurt is truly vicious: it says *I will get you back*. This kind of hurt is a sin. It is revenge. The second type of hurt is called a therapeutic hurt: it says, *I care about you and I care about me. I cannot continue to enable you to keep using this type of behavior.* An example is taking the keys away from your son when he has been drinking. He is hurt and angry and lashes out at you, which may hurt you, but you have done the caring thing by disciplining him. You are willing to let him be angry at you and feel hurt by the discipline, so that he will learn to stay within healthy boundaries.

Healthy boundaries create a balanced life. There was a balance to Jesus' life through a certain kind of moderation. Not a limitation on his love, compassion, mercy, and forgiveness, but moderation in honoring His own physical, emotional, and spiritual needs. His body was indeed the temple of the Holy Spirit just as ours is. Often to the disciples' and crowds' dismay, Jesus drew away in order to refresh His body and renew His spirit.

Taking responsibility means we are to know and accept our vulnerability, our limits, our weaknesses, and our desires. It means learning what your boundaries are, where you begin, and where another ends. Honor the pace of grace, as you trust God to transform you in His time. The joy and pleasure you experience far outweighs going outside God's boundaries.

5. **If you were in the same situation with your cousin, journal your thoughts about how you would feel about helping him again? What could you really do or not do?**

## Jesus Showed Us Healthy Boundaries

As we have seen, Christ-like help has boundaries. The story of the Good Samaritan illustrates how someone was able to help a man in distress; but at the same time, maintain his boundaries and not become enmeshed with the man's tragedy. You probably know what the Good Samaritan did (or please take a few minutes to read Luke 10:30-37). Let's look at what the Good Samaritan did not do. He didn't cancel his business trip. He didn't stay until the badly wounded man recovered, nor did he consider himself the only source of help. He entrusted the injured man to another's care. He was then able to carry out his own responsibilities by dividing the burden. He didn't return until he had finished his business.

We can also see that the Good Samaritan didn't turn his life upside down to solve this man's extended problems. He didn't give the man money to replace what he'd lost. He didn't help him find and prosecute his assailants. He didn't start an anti-crime campaign or a fund drive for crime victims. In short, he saw a need, did what he could do, involved others, but didn't abandon his own responsibilities in the wake of someone else's crisis. The Good Samaritan maintained his own boundaries and did not invade the injured man's boundaries. Christ-like help has healthy boundaries.

Christ-like help honors God's will before another's needs or desires. We are not called to react to other people's agendas. Mary and Martha wanted Jesus to come immediately to heal their brother Lazarus. Even though Jesus loved Mary and Martha, He stayed where He was two more days and, as a result, Lazarus died. Jesus did not even send any explanation to Mary and Martha to justify His decision. Jesus delayed so that His friend would die — it was His Father's will "for God's glory so that God's Son may be glorified through it." (John 11:1-45) Jesus did not equate serving others with pleasing others.

Once, while I was teaching a class about boundaries, a young mother was wrestling with what to do regarding one of her children. "He is just so scattered. He leaves his homework at home and I get in the car and take it to him. He leaves his lunch money at home and I take it to him. Several times a week I am running things he forgot to the school. What am I to do? I feel so guilty if I do not take him what he needs." As I heard her need to do so much for her son, I remembered how Jesus did not do everything that everyone wanted. I said, "Have you ever considered that doing *nothing* is doing *something*? Not taking the items to your son is doing something. It is teaching him you cannot always be available for him as you too have things to manage in your own life."

Like Jesus, sometimes our *not* doing something for a person is truly doing something for them. And what is that? We help them take ownership of what is within their boundaries to care for. We teach them that others have boundaries also. Our goal is to help them stand on their own and not expect to live expecting others to always rescue them. Jesus Himself did not cure every illness or meet every need when He lived on earth in a physical body. We are called to help, but we must have godly limits. The Holy Spirit helps us moderate between being a godly helper of others and a compassionate caretaker of ourselves as well.

6. **Is there a relationship in your life needing healthy boundaries? How can you set these boundaries? Pray and journal about this.**

## Honoring Boundaries Set by Others

Both God the Father and Jesus show us a model for respecting boundaries set by others. Jesus respected the rich young ruler's decision to walk away from eternal life. Jesus did not spend hours trying to win him. Jesus let him go. (Luke 18:18-25) Jesus allowed him to live with his choice and retain responsibility for his decision. People often ask why God allows pain and suffering. They protest, "God can do anything He wants, so why doesn't He fix this?" They may not even be sure He exists, but surely He is at fault when someone suffers. Is this really true? Can God do anything He wants? He has boundaries, too. He does nothing outside of His perfect character. Can He lie? He does not lie because He is truth. Can He burst through our wills and make us become Christians? He does not make us become Christians because He gives us a free will to choose. Nothing is too hard for our God, but this does not mean He breaks His own boundaries to do it. He keeps true to His character.

Jesus deeply desired that Israel would accept Him as their messiah, saying, "O Jerusalem, O Jerusalem, murdering the prophets and stoning those who are sent to you! How often would I have gathered your children together as a mother fowl gathers her brood under her wings and you refused." (Matthew 23:37) Jesus did not force Israel to accept Him. If we do not want Him in our lives and don't want His help, God will not cross our boundaries. He allows us to choose. We have to invite Him to be involved in our lives, our work, our schools, and our communities. Larry King once asked Billy Graham's daughter Anne, "Where was God on 9/11?" Her response went something like this: "God is not welcomed in our schools and for the most part, in our society. He has been removed. He will not violate our free will. If we don't want Him in our life or country, He honors our boundaries. We have to invite Him to protect and watch over our families, cities and country."

Some call this event God's judgment. Looking from another perspective, we might say God honored the boundaries set by others. The natural consequence of excluding Almighty God from various areas of our lives is He removes His hand of protection. Once we take over control of our situation, we forfeit God's control and step outside His boundaries for us. When we tell God in so many words, "I couldn't care less about You," a God-shaped vacuum is left in our lives and in our society, making us vulnerable to whatever would come to fill that vacuum. In this vacuum, humanism, atheism, and all the other *-isms* can proliferate. God honors the boundaries He has allowed us to set, and when we push Him out, He leaves and we will suffer the consequences of our choices.

**7. Do you honor the boundaries set by others in your life? Journal about a recent example.**

**8. Are there people in your life or have there been people in your life who walked all over your boundaries? How do you feel about this?**

## Internal Boundaries with Yourself

Setting internal boundaries with yourself is as important as setting external boundaries with others. Internal boundaries and self-control are one and the same. You might have heard someone say, "He (or she) is an adult child." When there is a wounded child inside of us, we find that this wounded child often over reacts in seemingly benign circumstances. Once the person understands his own dynamic, it is incumbent upon the adult to set boundaries with the wounded child. The adult acts on behalf of the wounded child within by going to God for power from the Holy Spirit. The adult relies on God to show how to select appropriate and healthy ways of dealing with the issue at hand.

Two very common areas in which we can hurt ourselves and others need to be understood: *spins* and *idols*. Being aware of these areas helps you discern when and if you have slipped into either. Loving yourself includes awareness of the pits you often fall into and so you can surrender them to God to change you and keep you within His boundaries.

131

**9. Journal about areas where you exercise self control and areas where you need healthy boundaries with yourself.**

## Harming Yourself and Others with Spins

What are spins? I've noticed this powerful dynamic working within most of the clients I counsel. Most of their time is spent trying to read the mind of a boyfriend, husband, friend or boss. They are forever trying to figure out the motives of the other person without including that person in the discussion. *Why did she do thus and so? What was he thinking when he did or said this and that?*

Let's say some type of relational issue has developed between my client and someone they care about. They want to use the counseling session asking what I think is happening regarding the latest episode between the two of them. No matter how many times I say we cannot read the other's mind, session after session they continue their focus on trying to figure out the other person. They seem to believe my training equips me to put the pieces together and give a definitive explanation.

Outside the session they may spend hours mulling over and talking with friends about what the other person might have been thinking, feeling, and what their real motive was. At some level they believe if they discuss it enough, clarity will come. If indeed the person believes they have clarity, in my experience they very rarely have the truth. They more than likely now believe a lie. I call this dynamic *putting a spin* on what someone said or did.

Our spins are similar to the way politicians and the media take an event and conjure up an explanation of what they think is going on in the life and mind of another. We too conjure up beliefs that take us out of the realm of reality and into the made up realm of our imaginations. These spins are based on assumptions, not facts. Our emotions, and often our actions, follow what our imaginations determine to be truth. Anytime we are not facing reality and are making up facts, we are headed for a cycle of relational madness of some magnitude.

An example of *spin*: John has not yet told anyone at the office he is undergoing tests to determine what is physically wrong with him. Because of his concern, he has been unusually quiet at the office. Today his doctor informed John he does indeed have cancer and will need chemotherapy. He comes back to work and is overcome with fear. His good buddy, Jack, walks up and begins talking about the crazy date he had this past weekend. John is unresponsive. Jack picks up on this and spins it in his mind: "John surely doesn't want to be bothered with me. In fact, he has been acting this way all month. I was going to ask him to lunch, but not now. If he is going to be this way, I'll just butt out." As the feeling of perceived rejection swells, it turns to anger and Jack walks away. His spin can be doubly painful for Jack if he has a history of rejection issues from his family.

What has just happened? First of all, Jack is spinning the situation. Jack told himself a lie: "John doesn't want a relationship with me." John never actually said anything to substantiate this! Secondly, Jack has just cut himself off from a friend who needs him now more than ever. And thirdly, he decides to hang his head and feel sorry for himself. He feels rejected and angry at John. His future with John has taken a turn. He and John probably will not be as close again unless this is straightened out. Now John will feel rejected by Jack and not know why.

What is reality? None of the above is reality. The only reality is that Jack has denied himself a good friendship. He has missed a great opportunity to become closer and minister to a hurting friend because he has misread the situation. Jack walked away sad, hurt, feeling rejected and angry because of what he thinks John did to him. John has not done anything to him. If Jack is like most people, the story does not end here. Jack talks to some office workers and spins the situation for them. "John has a burr under his saddle. He is ignoring me. What's wrong with him?" Others say, "Yeah, he has been really unsociable lately." Jack gets some people to sympathize with him. What is Jack doing? He is sinning against another and himself. Jack told himself a lie, involved others in his lie, and disparaged a friend all because he did not check out his hypothesis and get the facts.

When checking a hypothesis, Jack might have said something like, "John, I have noticed over these past few weeks you seem preoccupied and I feel you might be upset with me for some reason. Is there something I have done to offend you?" John then could tell him what is going on in his life. God calls us to be committed to truth and to reality. When we live in reality, we are taking care of and loving ourselves and others.

Spinning runs rampant in our society. I would venture to say the majority of social and work-related conversations focus on questions such as: *What do you think Sally meant when she said she is going to talk with the CEO? Why is George not dating Sarah any more? Did you know Bill was fired? What do you think happened?* These are legitimate interests, but what do we do with the questions? Either singularly or with a group we come up with the answers. Putting bits and pieces together, we weave a hypothesis, take it as fact, believe the lie we have created, and live by it. The person you are spinning is the only one who has the facts. All we are doing is whistling in the wind and that whistling is called slander. When we slander we smear, malign and disparage another. This is sin.

The slander leads to the defamation of a person's character based on hypotheses that are never checked out with the person in question. When we believe our own conclusions (lies), we can adversely impact the course of another person's life. And they never even know why their relational or work dynamics have taken a turn for the worse. Deception has moved in, all in the name of trying to figure out the heart of a person without going to the person directly. The end result of putting spins on events is to dig a deep hole of anguish for yourself and the other person.

A person's false reality can also become a self-fulfilling prophecy that works against them. We take a hypothesis, call it truth, and feed it to ourselves. This hypothesis is not reality, but we live and feel and act as if it is truth, hurting our relationships and ourselves. We are not loving ourselves when we cooperate with this type of thinking and discourse. We need to set an internal boundary with ourselves.

I was caught up in this cycle of thinking for years. When I was first married, I got in touch with my anger. I had never considered myself an angry person. My anger escalated into rage. I spent years raging at my husband. Why? The needy part of me was demanding attention in a manner I thought was appropriate. I was convinced my husband was intentionally withholding what I needed.

I put spins on everything. *He is late tonight. He found someone else. He is not sharing with me his inner life. He is withholding on purpose. He wants to hurt me. He doesn't love me. He doesn't want me around. He doesn't respect me. Why is he purposely doing this to me?* I tried to fix him and he wouldn't be fixed. I played the victim for years, trying to get his attention. I kept myself and the family upset most of the time with my spins. This did not need to be. Due to my lack of knowledge about self-defeating, needy thinking and behavior, I was going down with the ship and taking the family with me.

Eventually, I understood. He was not withholding what I wanted. He did not have within him what I was demanding. It wasn't that he would not give what I wanted; it was that he could not. We were both operating on empty. One day I asked my therapist when would I ever stop being so angry. She replied, "When you get sick and tired of being sick and tired, you will give it up." I eventually did get sick and tired and God began to help me let go of my expectations and stop listening to my own spins regarding what I thought might be happening. God helped me heal and depend on Him and my Christian friends for acceptance and validation.

**10. Journal about a time when you put a spin on some situation. In what ways did you unnecessarily stir yourself up with emotions?**

### *Harming Yourself with Idols*

As we come to the close of this chapter, I want to share another insight that will help with understanding the need to set some internal boundaries with yourself. I learned that all the worrying and fretting I did about my family exhibited a lack of trust in God's ability. It spoke volumes about my walk with the Lord in this area of my life. I saw not only that I didn't trust God, but I also made an idol out of my worrying. I especially made an idol out of my husband. Not an idol I worshiped, but one I obsessed over and spent most of my time and energy trying to fix.

Idols and addictions are, if not the same, then very similar in function. Any *addiction* is defined as the state of being enslaved to a habit or practice, or to something or someone that is psychologically or physically habit-forming, with features of compulsions, cravings, and yearnings. An *idol* is defined by Scripture as anything taking God's place in our lives. It can also be defined as any person or thing regarded with blind admiration, adoration, or devotion. The addicted person spends large portions of their time thinking and obsessing about how to obtain the thing or person they need.

They believe they can not live without the object desired. Because of the addiction, their families, their friends, and their work are at risk.

Many different things or activities can become addictions or idols for us. We may have a computer addiction. Computers are wonderful, but when we spend so much time on them, with little to no intimate communication with family members, then there is an addiction taking hold (becoming an idol). Disconnection and distance move in between the family members. There is a strong drive within the person to get on the computer. This dynamic can happen with anything: golf, jogging, a boyfriend, Bible study, children, gardening, sugar, or pornography. Each can be an addiction or idol. Our idol not only takes us away from family relations but also takes precedence over God. Once our focus is on the thing we are obsessing over, our focus is off God in this area of our lives. The thing or activity in itself may not be bad, but our connection with it becomes bad for us.

As a wife with learned helplessness, and little regard for herself, the thing I craved, obsessed over and spent large portions of time trying to get at the expense of my family, was my husband's validation. My mind was forever focused on wanting to do, to get, to fix, to be with, or to have the thing I so longed for. Slowly, this idol attitude began to adversely affect me, my husband, and the children. It came out mainly in rage. I knew my rage was sin but I was trapped in my own history (or so I thought).

In reality I was blocking God's hand in the situation. I needed to let go of these drives and let God work on me. When we try to extract something out of another person the opposite of what we so desperately want is taking place. We are destroying the very relationship or thing we want so badly. I personally believe God will not work no matter how much we pray as long as we are still trying to fix the other person. We need to surrender the thing or person and give up on fixing. I do not guarantee you will get what you thought you wanted, but what you do get is peace inside your soul. All the toil and angst is gone. Over time God healed my rage. The anger backed down into a normal range. I learned how to talk out my anger and *care-front* (caringly confront) my husband with respect for him and respect for myself. Has anything changed? He is a kinder and gentler husband now.

When I begin to fret about someone or something, I realize I am beginning to dig a hole for myself. I can choose to stop digging and ask the Lord to do what I cannot do: "I realize I do not trust You, Lord, in this situation. I need Your strength to help my unbelief. I want to trust You totally. I cannot fix or change another person so I am entrusting my desires to You. Thank You for exchanging my weakness with Your strength. Amen."

**11. Do you recognize an idol/addiction you need to surrender? What is it? Journal your feelings about an idol you have recognized in your life.**

## In Summary

We need healthy boundaries. We see that God has boundaries, and Jesus showed His use of boundaries when He was here on earth. God wants us to have healthy boundaries that reflect His values for us. Christian self-sacrifice and codependency look a lot alike, but codependency has no boundaries when it comes to helping other people. When we are codependent, we become resentful, angry, and burned out. Christian self-sacrifice has boundaries so that we serve one another in love without taking complete responsibility for the other person. These are external boundaries between ourselves and others.

We also need to set internal boundaries with ourselves. One of those internal boundaries is to be aware when we put spins on what we think is going on with another person. Our spins are only theories. We must get a reality check from the person and go from there with our relationship. We can also create idols of things or activities in our lives by making them too important, too close to our hearts. Idols and spins keep us stuck in a quagmire of frustration and grief. Give your idols to your Abba (Papa) who will set you free to love and to serve Him alone.

**Ask God to show you what He wants you to learn and do as a result of this chapter. Don't go on a witch hunt to fix everything in your life by yourself! When you ask Him, trust Him to show you what He wants you to surrender. Then surrender and walk inside His protection.**

# CHAPTER 7

# THE INNER JOURNEY

## *Is It All About Me?*

### *The Diamond*

*I sat in the case beside the most beautiful stone in the store. The sign between us said* Before and After. *Customers would grimace at me and smile at the beautiful stone beside me. It's his fault! If he weren't so beautiful, I would get more smiles. If the manager would just redirect the lights, then my facets would shine. Surely that saleslady could hang me on a necklace, where I would really shine.*

*One day the jeweler opened the case, removed the sign, seized me with tongs, and placed me on a dark mat. With a bright light he carefully examined me. He cut me over and over again. What a long and painful process! Soon he began polishing. I got so hot I felt like I was melting.*

*Today I stand on display right next to the finest stone in the store, except now I, too, am refined and beautiful. My facets catch every ray of light and throw them out to dance brilliantly all around.*

*All of my life I believed my darkness was caused by others. If only I had known that I just needed to spend some time in the jeweler's hands.*

By Ashley Wille

## A Disclaimer

In our Christian journey we all encounter painful situations that seem to be endless no matter how much we pray. We can be tempted to wonder if God is still there or if He really cares about our problems. We may fall back into judging ourselves and trying harder to fix our circumstances. Understanding how God has worked in the lives of others can help you better understand what God is doing during those long, dark days. You are loving yourself as you join in with God rather than fighting against Him.

Undeniably, God has the authoritative right to deal with each of us in any way He chooses. Yet there do seem to be some principles God uses as He works in our circumstances. I want to share with you how I perceive God most often works in my life and in my clients' lives. Know this is one way, not the only way God works.

When our prayers seem to be unanswered, in our agony we ask hard questions. "I know God is trying to teach me something in all of this, but I don't know what it is." Or, "Why is this happening to me? If only God would say *yes* to my prayer and come through, I could be at peace. I could rest." These questions are valid, but rarely do we find answers sufficient to give us peace. Often, we remain stuck in emotional and spiritual turmoil. But what if you better understood what was happening to you? If you had a better perspective, it could give you direction and hope. You must be steadfast not to judge or condemn yourself if you plan to take this *inside-out journey*. Otherwise this process can be riddled with pain and guilt rather than anticipation and faith in God's ability to change and deliver you.

## An Inner Journey with the Lord

Having been a Christian for many years, I've learned a lot, grown a lot, and been confused a lot. It took me a long time to realize God is more interested in my internal growth than in my external circumstances. I wanted outside-in fixes to my situations. The mantra of my life was: "Rescue me!" I cried out to my parents, my husband, and God. I thought I had to be rescued from whatever was causing me anxiety, depression, or pain. Praying about our circumstances is definitely biblical; however, I believe God looks at our hearts and then determines how He will work uniquely within each of us. In my case, I believe God knew my need to be rescued was far too disproportionate to what a healthy response to life might be. I needed an inside-out fix. He wanted me to stand in His strength rather than look to another.

The frustration I felt with my husband remained during the time one of our two sons became involved with drugs. No matter how much I prayed, my husband wasn't changing and my son wasn't changing. "God what are You doing? I need Your deliverance. Please change my husband. Please change my son." Nothing changed.

I was caught in what St. John of the Cross called *the dark night of the soul.* I felt overwhelmed and out of touch with God. Hopelessness and helplessness invaded every part of my soul. I believed the pain would never stop. You too may recognize a situation that has brought you to feeling this way. Coming to the end of ourselves is an out-of-control experience and we want control! We can be reassured by realizing this seems to be a common Christian experience, and God knows everything that will happen to us. In this state, we have two choices: turn to God and cooperate with Him, or turn away from Him.

God uses this time to draw us into a deeper walk with Him and often to prepare us for *relational ministry* either in a professional or lay capacity. When we open our hearts to God, He becomes the center of our lives. During this time we learn to connect with our own hearts and pain without judgment, preparing us for ministry to others in pain.

I discovered David's plea to God, "Search me [thoroughly], O God, and know my heart! Try me and know my thoughts! And see if there is any wicked or hurtful way in me, and lead me in the way everlasting." (Psalm 139:23-24) The Holy Spirit convinced me that I, like David, needed an *inner journey* with the Lord. I made an appointment with a Christian therapist to help me on that journey.

A Christian who has been through their own *dark night journey* can listen and not give premature advice or Bible verses. We need someone to sit with us in our confusion and listen to us as we work through our pain and come to an understanding of our own dynamics that have trapped us for years. God has given us Himself, His Son, the Holy Spirit, His Word and the Body of Christ (the true Christian community). God often gives us another Christian to walk with us through this dark night, someone who has experienced the *inside-out principle* and knows first-hand its precious results.

**1. Journal what you have or have not experienced of the inner journey. What have you learned from your inner journey?**

### The Inside-Out Principle

The inside-out principle is the second most important principle to know next to not judging ourselves. Heeding these two principles set us free from what holds us back from being all God created us to be. Dr. Henry Brandt, a pioneer of biblical counseling, makes clear this *inside-out principle* when he said, *"It is not your circumstance that creates the pain. It is your circumstance that brings up who you are."* Our circumstances bring up who we really are? Ouch! A distressing situation brings up our chronic, non-medically induced anxiety, depression, anger, fear, sadness, and self-soothing addictions that are already within us. Our reactions to these external triggers give us a good look into ourselves.

Our strong emotions are a window to our souls. The *inside-out principle* maintains that our adverse circumstances allow those things—things of which God is aware but we are not—to rise into our emotions and into our awareness for the purpose of showing us what needs healing. These chronic overreactions are to be considered red flags God is waving, declaring: "This is what I want to change and heal within you if you will let Me." If we do not pay attention to these warnings, our pain will go on and our lives will stay on hold right where we are.

**2. What is the Inside-Out principle? Journal your feelings and thoughts about the Inside-Out principle working in your life?**

## The Path of the Inner Journey

Taking the *inner journey*, being willing to discover and know our own hearts, is a path seldom chosen. It is often *the road less traveled.* For 38 years I avoided this path. I lived in an outside-in fix-me world that kept me stuck in behaviors that did not glorify the Lord. Many of our prayers are not answered because we avoid this path and live in the hope of an outside-in fix.

### *We Do Not Know Our Own Hearts*

In his book, *Understanding Who You Are,* Cecil Osborn asks, "If you are not honest with yourself; how can you be honest with God? And if you cannot be honest with God, how can He help you?" We must discover the hidden things of our heart, be honest with ourselves, and then be honest with God. When we are willing to commit to our reality and in turn bring that reality to God, God can heal us.

God knows our hearts (1 Samuel 16:7, Psalm 139) and He wants us to know our hearts, as well. If God were to immediately heal our external circumstance, we would not know our own hearts. We would not know from what toxic beliefs or wounds we had been delivered. The next time we encountered difficulty we would do the same things the same way. Because we didn't know our hearts, we would experience further pain. We would have learned nothing about our unhealthy emotions and behaviors.

God allows us to go to these places of emotional pain so we will give up on our self-sufficient way of doing things. Life becomes intolerable. In this intolerable place, God wants us to be like the prodigal son who recognized where he really was and decided to return to his father. God wants us to come to our senses and say, "I don't want to be here, continuing this behavior. I want to be with my heavenly Father!" We, too, must know our own hearts, come to the end of ourselves, and allow God to help us own our part of the emotional muck we find ourselves in.

Healing comes with awareness of the root of our pain. The Spirit of God cannot lead us to a place of healing when we are not even aware a root of some sort exists. We are to turn to God for understanding; remembering that regardless of what He shows me, "There is therefore now no condemnation for those who are in Christ Jesus." (Romans 8:1)

**3. Are you at a place where all your self-sufficient resources to fix a situation have run out? Are you yet aware of what needs to be healed within you? If so what is it? Journal your answers to these questions.**

## We Find Landmines

We each have our very own personal landmines, created in the past and hidden from our awareness. When someone unintentionally steps on one of our landmines, our intense reactions feel like a surprise landmine explosion. We do and say things that separate us from God, ourselves, and others. The person who stepped on our landmine has no idea what they have done, or what has just happened. They are bewildered. We believe with our hearts that the other person has willfully hurt us. This may not really be the case. The other person may have said something that could register a slight rise in emotions, but not to the degree we are experiencing them now. This strong overreaction indicates something needs healing within us.

As a graphic example, let's say we experience emotions on a scale of 1 to 10, with 1 being a very slight reaction and 10 being an over-the-top, very strong reaction. If we have attended to the wounds in our lives, when someone says or does something that crosses a boundary and so we think their action is inappropriate, our emotions might register a reaction between 1 and 5 on our emotional scale. A person experiencing an emotion in this range can stay in the present and address the situation in an adult manner. However, if we have numerous unhealed wounds and the exact same event happens, we will register a 9 or 10 reaction on our emotional scale. While the present situation may normally rate a 4 reaction for other people, in our unhealed state, the event adds a 6 from the past wounding to our present 4. We add 4 with 6 and we experience a 10 reaction! This dynamic may happen over and over again. The emotionally disproportionate reaction is truly out of our control. We can know God is purposely allowing the pain to surface so we will attend to it and bring it to Him.

**4. Describe a situation where someone stepped into your landmine and you over-reacted; or describe a situation where you stepped into a landmine and the other person over-reacted. What was the unhealed wound causing the explosion?**

### *Outside-In Fix: Blaming Others*

When I first began walking with the Lord, I was a babe drinking the milk of the Word. My prayers focused on others. I had difficulty seeing or recognizing what I needed in prayer. I saw my needs according to what was happening to those in and outside our family. If there was turmoil in our family, I earnestly prayed for the family member causing the turmoil. For years I would meet weekly with friends to pray for our families. All this seems appropriate, and it is. But what was my motive? Was it all that altruistic for me? Yes and no.

I now see what I did not realize then: I was believing a lie. The lie went something like this: "If you (the other person in my life), will stop doing *x*, *y*, and *z*, I will not feel this pain. Or, if you will do *a*, *b*, and *c*, I will be okay. You are not giving me what I need and what I want. My hurt and anger are your fault. Something is wrong with you! I must pray that you change. I know it is best for you to change." I believed my family members must change in order for my pain to change. All sorts of negative feelings, thoughts, and actions rose within me from what I considered *their* negative behaviors and *their* stubborn refusal to change. My problems were because of them. Thus, my prayers were all about them. This is another toxic lie: being at peace *depends* on

others being what I need them to be. If this were true, then
I am hopeless. This side of heaven, we will never be able to
completely live up to our expectations.

This type of blame game is as old as Adam and Eve.
Adam said, "The woman You gave to be with me, Lord, she
gave me the fruit." Then Eve said, "Oh, the serpent deceived
me." She implied, "It was the snake's fault!" Adam blamed
Eve and God, and Eve blamed the snake. (see Genesis 3)
This *Adam and Eve Syndrome* blocks building a healthy relationship with God, self, and others. When we blame others
for our behavior, we don't take responsibility for the part we
may have played. Without knowing this, we can hold up or
delay God's answer that we are so desperately praying to
receive. The blame game also puts the blamed person on the
defense and creates an environment in which they will not
listen to us. If we want healing, we must not play the blame
game. We are to look to ourselves first to determine why this
person's behavior has so much power over us.

**5. Journal about how you have experienced the Adam
   and Eve Syndrome.**

### *Outside-In Fix: Praying for the Wrong Thing*

In my early days as a Christian, I met a new friend at a
Bible study who had become a Christian at about the same
time as I had. As we got to know each other, I saw how she
seemed overly preoccupied with her need for a house. She
and her husband were having problems. She was sure if they
could get out of their small apartment with their two children and buy a house they would be fine. She prayed and
prayed for a new home. When a new home did not come,
she dropped out of the Bible study and I lost track of her. I
believe with all my heart God was trying to tell her, "Your
priorities are wrong. A house is not the answer to finding

peace. I Am. And I want to heal your marriage by changing and healing you." But her heart was set on getting a house, thinking this would bring them peace. I later learned they had bought a house, but the marriage still dissolved. Sometimes we pray for the wrong thing, and we miss what God really wants to do for us.

**6. Do you recall a time when you were praying for the wrong thing? How did God show you this?**

### *Outside-In Fix: Trying to Fix the Other Person*

Problems are part of life, and we spend much of our time finding solutions to them. But sometimes, we think we cannot tolerate the internal turmoil we feel in the situation. We focus everything on the person in this situation who we think *has to be fixed*. I spent years trying to fix my outside circumstances and railing at those who would not change. One day, I finally entered my Christian therapist's office, saying with great resolve, "I have had it! I don't care if my circumstances ever change. *I just want to be able to live life to its fullest within my circumstances.*" I believe it was at this point God saw I finally had the proverbial horse in front of the cart—just where it should be. He and I were finally on the same page; we were able to begin walking together toward His Sabbath rest as I began to learn how to live at peace *within* my circumstances.

God answered the cry of my heart. Why? Because I had given up on fixing others and began to understand God wanted to heal something in my life. Instead of focusing on changing the other person, I focused on my part in the situation. When we are frantically grasping to fix another person, God allows us to beat our heads against the wall for as long as it takes for our hearts to come in line with His will. God wants to heal me, and He works with me to bring healing.

The only person God gives us permission to fix is ourselves and we can't even do that without His intervention.

**7. Is there someone in your life right now whom you are trying to fix? Who is it? How is trying to fix them impacting you?**

### We Ask for What We Already Have

Often we pray and beg God to give us blessings we already have. As we have discussed, we already have everything that pertains to life and godliness. Ephesians 1:3 says, "Praise be to the God and Father of our Lord Jesus Christ, who has blessed us in the heavenly places with every spiritual blessing in Christ Jesus."

For years I wondered why night after night as a teen I would beg God to forgive me for my sins, yet nothing happened. Guilt—with non-stop self-persecution—stayed with me. As an adult, I wondered, "Why didn't You answer me, God? I know my heart was right. I was repentant for my sins." Then I discovered the truth. God *did* forgive me. Each time I begged, He forgave me. I just did not know He forgave me. This is the reason we need to know what God has already given us, so Satan can not use our ignorance to deceive us and keep us suffering. As I shared this with a client, she told me that for years she, too, had begged God to seal her with the Holy Spirit. Eventually she discovered He did that at the moment of her committing to Jesus. For years she didn't understand she was *already* sealed.

Once I was wrestling with God and myself about a decision I needed to make. I kept asking for wisdom and direction, feeling I was not receiving it. One day I read, "If any of you is deficient in wisdom, let him ask of the giving God [Who gives] to everyone liberally and ungrudgingly, without reproaching or fault finding, and it will be given him." (James

1:5) I realized that *God says if I ask for wisdom He will give it to me.* Simple enough! I got up off my knees and walked out knowing I had God's wisdom. Could I verbalize it at that moment? No. But if God said He gave it to me, then I knew that when the moment came to use that wisdom, it would be there. I worried no more.

Many of us beg for more faith. Jesus said, "If you had faith [trust and confidence in God] even [so small] like a grain of mustard seed, you could say to this mulberry tree, be pulled up by the roots, and be planted in the sea, and it would obey you." (Luke 17:6) I often question clients who say they don't have enough faith by asking, "Do you believe you have faith comparable to this tiniest of all seeds, the mustard seed?" Most believe they do. Then I say, "Jesus said this is enough faith to say to a tree, 'Be pulled up and be planted in the sea.' This seems like enough faith to me." God often uses our circumstances to show us we need to take hold of what we already have, but we are not using. When we pray for faith, we may want to consider instead if we are really trusting in the promises of God.

8. **Have you experienced asking for something God has already given to you, and then coming to understand He has already given you His gift? Journal about this.**

## Suffering Can Be Redemptive

The *inner journey* brings redemption to your suffering. Webster's Dictionary defines *redeem* as: *to buy back; to free from what distresses or harms, from captivity by payment of ransom, or from the consequences of sin.* Galatians 4:4-5 reminds us, "...God sent His Son, born of a woman, born subject to [the regulations of] the Law, to purchase the freedom of [to ransom, to *redeem*, to atone for] those who were subject to the Law, that we might be adopted and have sonship conferred upon us [and be recognized as God's sons]." God redeemed us through His Son: He wants to free us from bondage. God is love: in love He extends grace through His Son, who said, "The Spirit of the Lord is upon me, because He anointed me to preach good tidings to the poor: He hath sent me to proclaim *release to the captives, and recovering of sight to the blind, to set at liberty them that are bruised, to proclaim the acceptable year of the Lord.*" (Luke 4:18, *emphasis mine*) As we allow Him to work from the inside out, this promise becomes real: "All things work together for good for those who love the Lord and are called according to His purpose." (Romans 8:28)

The saga of Joseph is a good example of God redeeming a very bad situation. (see Genesis 33- 45) Joseph's ten brothers sell him into slavery as a young teen. Years later they come for help to Egypt's ruler serving just under the Pharaoh during an insufferable famine. They don't recognize this is Joseph, their brother. When Joseph finally reveals who he is, he also tells his brothers, "What you meant for evil, God has turned to good." (see Genesis 50:19-20) The redemptive good was that over the years while a slave, Joseph found favor with people of high standing. Ultimately he became the second-in-command in Egypt. Because of this position, Joseph was able to save his brothers, his father, and their families from starvation and to preserve the lineage of Jesus. From Joseph's anguish God brought good. His suffering was redeemed by God: not only for Joseph's good, but for God's glory and ultimately our salvation.

**9. Has God allowed suffering in your life? Have you seen how He will work for your good in this? Journal your thoughts about your suffering.**

## Preparation for Ministry

In her book, *Dark Night Journey*, Sandra Cronk states, "This inward formation is more important than the outward training in ministry. Ministry is not a task but a way of being in the world." We can know Bible verses in our head, which is necessary, but the truths of scripture must be transferred into our hearts and into our reality. The dark night journey does just that. As we come to radical dependence on God, we know in the depth of our being that without God in every aspect of our lives, we will not be able to function in this world. A true humility is worked into our souls. We know in the depth of our being that God is God and we are not. From within, a controlled power reaches out in the name of Christ to the lost and to the church. As this radical dependence fills our souls, God's grace shouts His love and acceptance for us and in turn for others also.

Cronk continues, "These people (the dark night journeyers) are the ones needed to lead the church. They are the ones who can speak to a dying world in the midst of their failures and brokenness and not be paralyzed by a sense of anger at these people for not living up to our visions." Matthew 9:36 says, "When He (Jesus) saw the throngs, He was moved with pity and sympathy for them, because they were bewildered [harassed and distressed and dejected and helpless], like sheep without a shepherd." We, too, become moved by compassion for the hurting because we, too, have been where they are. We bring the wounded to our God who heals. When we have been emptied of our desire to control, the Shepherd of eternal life can use us to lead the lost and the church to Him!

10. **Have you taken a dark night journey? What did you learn in it? Has God given you a place of ministry as a result?**

## Jane's Story

Jane had a tough childhood. Her stepfather relentlessly belittled and yelled at her. She suffered shame and rejection. Now she is an adult and a Christian. She does well with most people; she really enjoys them. Occasionally she meets a person she fears. She does not know why. Her boss is one of these people. One day her boss called Jane into his office. As they discussed a particular project, his voice became louder and louder (possibly with enthusiasm) until Jane felt he was angry. Jane began to feel like a little girl. Out of nowhere, uncontrollable tears began to flow down her cheeks. She was embarrassed, frightened and wanted to get away from him as quickly as possible.

Since that time, every day as Jane wakes up, dresses, and drives into work, anxiety overtakes her. She hates her job and wants to quit. What is happening to Jane? The wounds of her past are not healed. She doesn't connect her past wounds with her present actions and feelings. The panic of past fears, living with her stepfather, is recreated as she drives to work fearing her boss. When she believed her boss was angry with her, she instantly went back in time to being a little girl, cowering, backing away, and crying as her stepfather berated her. She feels the shame and rejection of her childhood, coupled with the terror of the anger she feels from her boss. She acts the way she did as a child. She begins to cry.

Jane has prayed over and over again for God to help her stop being so frightened. There is no release. What is happening to Jane? Jane may label herself an inferior Christian, and feel she is not worthy of help. She may believe she has to have stronger faith to get God's attention. But if she can understand that her emotional overreactions are signals from God to get her attention, then she can begin to work together with God towards change and healing.

155

God is like a doctor who wants to heal the root of the problem, not just the symptoms. Jane may want automatic healing from her anxiety, but God allows this repeated pain because He is trying to tell her there is unfinished business in her life that needs to be attended to. Jane may choose to judge herself and say, "What is wrong with me? I am just an emotional basket case. My boss probably will never advance me. I am so stupid!" But what if she skips the judgment and goes immediately to God to look for redemption from the chaos created by her family of origin? Owning this recurring dynamic, she may ask God, "Help me understand the origins of these reactions. Show me what You know about me that I don't know about myself. Work on my inner woman and change me. I am willing to go on an *inner journey* with You, Lord." She may feel truly hopeless on her own, but she can find real hope in our God who heals.

When she finds hope in God, she is not trapped into believing she must quit her job. She may change jobs after she is healed and can determine if her relationship with her boss really was toxic or not. Leaving before allowing God to heal her only prolongs her healing because she will take her wounds with her into new work settings. Her prayer is, "Lord, this scenario keeps happening to me. I can't change myself. I have tried. My life is out of control in this area. If anything changes, it will be because You change me. I am turning my pain and my reactions over to You, Lord. I trust You to reveal what triggers me and then help me when tempted to react this way again."

She and God are working together. If she starts to take back her fear of someone else's anger she may react this way again. If she does, Jane remembers to not judge herself and turn it over to the Lord again. She does this as many times as necessary. Why does she do this? She has come to the end of trying to fix her overwhelming feelings and actions. She will not take the pain back because to take it back means more pain. Thus, she volleys the problem back to God each time her fear of another's anger rises within her. She reminds herself where the fear is really coming from: her stepfather's sins against her.

**11. How can you identify with Jane's story? Do you need to find a Christian friend to walk with you in your inner journey?**

## In Summary

God's commitment to us is relentless. We are to be confident God will never give up on us, even if we give up on Him. God promises us: "He who began a good work in you will continue until the day of Jesus Christ [right up to the time of His return], developing [that good work] and perfecting and bringing it to full completion in you." (Philippians 1:6)

When life seems to blow up in your face, know God desires to redeem this pain for your good and His glory. He wants to work from the inside out. You can choose to look to God and then take an inner journey with Him to discover what your triggers are and how they came into being. Whatever you discover there, know God is no longer judging you. You have already been judged upon accepting Jesus as your Lord and Savior and the verdict was: "Not guilty!" God, in His love and mercy, desires to take your miserable situation and work it out for your good. Most of the time that good will happen inside of you, but it may also lead to outward changes.

In His mercy God will not allow negative attitudes, thought patterns, false beliefs, or unhealthy actions to continue to control you, especially the ones you are not even aware of. He knows Satan is taking you at will. God does not want you to continue being blindsided by the enemy. God wants you free from any bondage.

When we sense our countenance has changed from one of peace to unpleasant emotional feelings and/or actions, this is our signal to stop, take notice and own what is going on within us. Diligently watch for any intensity of pain or loss of peace you experience during the day. With God, examine your internal realities then determine if the loss of your peace is a result of a sin, a wound, or an embedded lie. Take the time to deal with whatever you discover. "What is going on within me, Lord? What do You want me to know about my overreaction, or my painful emotions in this situation? Where in my past did this reaction first begin?"

**Journal about what this means for you: "He who did not spare his own Son, but gave him up for us all – how will he not also, along with him, graciously give us all things?" (Romans 8:32)**

# CHAPTER 8

# STRENGTH IN WEAKNESS

## *Good News?*

### *The Butterfly*

*I am fragile. I am slow. I float from flower to flower. The currents carry me along and the sun heats my wings so I can fly. I follow the fragrances that capture my senses. My beauty lies in the strength of my Creator who gives me life.*

*By Ashley Wille*

*W*eakness can be defined as *flawed, lacking*, and *inadequate.* As Americans we run from weaknesses, because we see weakness as a defect. We go to great lengths to hide our weaknesses, because they are liabilities and they make us vulnerable. If our weaknesses are exposed, we often feel emotionally out of control. We see others as having power over us. We don't readily identify with the phrase *strength in weakness.* Weakness is not great news for us and strength in weakness seems like an oxymoron.

My clients want me to help them be stronger. One client asked during her first session, "You are going to help me be stronger, aren't you?" I smiled and said gently, "No, I am going to help you accept your weaknesses." She had not expected to hear this. The idea of accepting your weaknesses was foreign to her and possibly may be foreign to you, as well. In scripture we discover weakness described as strength. How can this be? My client did not know what Paul and I knew. God set in place a *Strength- in-Weakness principle* that operates on our behalf. Accepting this principle will bring about more freedom and God Esteem.

Helping a person become stronger in *self* is in direct opposition to the Word of God. Christianity teaches we humans are to come to a place where we acknowledge and embrace our inability to live out God's directives in our lives. This weakness is intended to move us closer to God in order for us to live in His strength, a divine strength. Paul prays for Christians "that He [God] would grant you, according to the riches of His glory, to be strengthened with power through His Spirit in the inner man." (Ephesians 3:16) That strength comes to us through the power of the Holy Spirit who resides within each Christian. Having your inner man/ woman strengthened by the Holy Spirit in those places you know are weak, brings rest and peace to your soul.

Just before he returned to heaven, Jesus told his disciples, "But you shall receive power [ability, efficiency, and might] when the Holy Spirit has come upon you, and you shall be My witnesses in Jerusalem and all Judea and Samaria and to the ends [the very bounds] of the earth." (Romans 5:1) God sent the Holy Spirit to the first disciples on Pentecost, and He gives us his Holy Spirit when we receive Jesus as our Savior. Romans15:13 says, "May the God of your hope so fill you with all joy and peace in believing [through the experience of your faith] that by the power of the Holy Spirit you may abound and be overflowing [bubbling over] with hope." When you first believed, the Holy Spirit immediately gives you bubbling-over hope and His power.

Jesus died for our sins—past, present, and future. The Holy Spirit was sent to earth to indwell and aid the believer while we are here on earth. The Holy Spirit can and will live Jesus' resurrected life in and through us, if we allow Him. God wants us to accept the Holy Spirit's power within us. And there's the rub. We have to admit we need help. There seems to be a Strength-in-Weakness principle at work here.

**1. What does weakness mean to you? What is the Holy Spirit's role in your life?**

## Too Strong, or Too Weak?

If we want to understand the Strength-in-Weakness principle, we can start by looking at the way people usually see their own strengths. People often see themselves in one of two categories. Some see themselves as extremely capable and strong. Others see themselves as weak and not capable at all. Seeing oneself in either of these ways negatively impacts our walk with the Lord.

The first type is the strong, self-assured person who believes, "I have answers, let me help you." They are usually competitive and lean on their own abilities to make it through life. We call these people codependent/independent types. They need themselves, and act as though they need no one else. The childhood circumstances of the codependent/ independent person may have revolved around a sick sibling in the family, an alcoholic father, party parents who were not present for the child, uninvolved working parents, or parents who went through the process of divorce. Because of the nature of their circumstances, these children learned to take care of themselves early in life. They took on adult responsibilities far too soon. For all practical purposes, they missed their childhood as they had to fend for themselves. They were either covertly or overtly given the responsibility for the wellbeing of the family. The burden of life was placed on their shoulders.

The second type is the codependent/ dependent style. They need others. They need people to advise them, to help them, to direct them. They developed learned helplessness in childhood. This is a helplessness that was inadvertently internalized from either overbearing parents or well-intentioned parents who over-protected the child from the world. These parents guided the child's life according to what they thought was right. The child learned not to have a say in the matter. The parents took charge of the majority of their child's decisions; by default, they failed to teach the child to think for him/herself.

Neither of these codependent types is effective in the kingdom of God. The codependent/independent, more grandiose type generally lives out of the flesh. Why? Because they have strong self confidence and self will that God wants to bring under His control. The codependent/ dependent type does not believe they can do anything; they have little idea of who they are. They often give up on being able to make life work for themselves or they can move into a mode of pretending they are sufficient. The title of this book, *Ending the War with Myself*, will probably attract codependent/dependent types who really feel overwhelmed by their internal struggles, or codependent/ independent types who have finally come to the end of all their self-efforts and in brokenness look to God for help.

In counseling the codependent/ dependent type understands and knows up front they are weak. They are more qualified than they could ever imagine to be used by God. Really knowing they are weak is an asset. The focus for them will be not judging themselves but moving towards trusting

God's ability to be strong on their behalf. Their weakness becomes the starting place for God to work in their lives.

The codependent/ independent type has a more difficult task. They must learn, sometimes through very difficult circumstances, they really do not have all the answers, are not as emotionally strong as they portray themselves to be, or have as much control over their lives as they may have believed in the past. The starting point for them will be in recognizing and owning their weaknesses.

**2. Would you say that you are the codependent/ independent or the codependent/ dependent? Journal about how this type has impacted your life.**

### *Give Up!*

Before his conversion experience, Paul is an example of the codependent/ independent type. In Romans 7, Paul describes his struggle with the flesh even after coming to Christ. The long list of Paul's achievements give him room to say, "I could boast." (see 2 Corinthians 11:21-29) In more than one of his letters, Paul tells how God used numerous circumstances to help humble the prideful Paul. Upon conversion Paul was blinded and had to be lead around by another: an out-of-control, humbling experience. God used a thorn in the flesh to remind Paul daily that he was not the one in charge. Paul ends his list of achievements by writing, "If I must boast, I will boast of the things that show my weakness." (2 Corinthians 11:30) It was in this place of humility that Paul was in a position to grow and be used in God's kingdom.

When we come to this out-of-control place in our lives, we are to recognize the positive possibilities that can come from being here. God desires we *give up* on ourselves ever living the Christian life or being able to fix someone else or, for that matter, to fix ourselves. When Paul asks God to remove the thorn in his flesh, Paul says: "And He [God] has said to me, 'My grace is sufficient for you, for power is perfected in weakness.' Most gladly, therefore, I would rather boast about my weaknesses, so that the power of Christ may dwell in me. Therefore, I am well content with weaknesses, with insults, with distresses, with persecutions, with difficulties, for Christ's sake; for when I am weak, then I am strong." (2 Corinthians 12:9-10)

**3. Have you given up on fixing yourself? How have you come to this place?**

## The Foolish, Weak, Inadequate Principle

God tells Paul His grace is sufficient for Paul's weakness. Paul responds, "I glory in my weakness because it is in my weakness that I am strong." (2 Corinthians 12:10) Why on earth, we cry, does God operate this way when our weaknesses can be so shameful or embarrassing? When we are at the end of our ability to resolve a matter and we own our inadequacy, God's strength can manifest itself in our inadequacy. It is like being on empty and coming to God to fill us up. We see all the discouraging issues we face, and this is when God does above and beyond what we think possible! Using our *Inside-Out principle*, He comes through for us with His strength in our weakness.

We experience a power and a peace we never thought possible. He manifests Himself through us to an unbelieving world, in spite of our weaknesses, to show He is strong on our behalf. We find ourselves being used of God. Over the centuries, "God has chosen the foolish things of this world to confound the wise, and chosen the weak things of the world to shame the things which are strong." (1 Corinthians 1:27) When you understand this is God's unassailable way to use us in His kingdom, then our weaknesses are not so daunting. Our weakness is not our enemy any more, but the place where God meets us in His power.

**4. What is your greatest weakness? How does God see this weakness in you? How can He use this weakness for His Glory and for your good?**

*Weak People God Used in Mighty Ways*

God has used many flawed, inadequate, and sinful people with all the human weaknesses we have. How could He use these types of people? God looks at their hearts rather than their capabilities.

When God asked Moses to go and lead His people out of Egypt, Moses pleaded with God to send someone else instead. Moses insisted he could not speak well enough to go to the Egyptian Pharaoh. God was angry with Moses, but He allowed Moses to take Aaron to do the speaking. (see Exodus 4:13-14) How embarrassing is that?

God used David, the youngest and smallest son of Jesse, to slay the giant Goliath instead of using the army of the Israelites. (see 1 Samuel 17)

Sampson had a weakness for women, as did David with Bathsheba. In fact, David had Bathsheba's husband, a general, put up on the front line of battle so he would be killed. This was murder, premeditated by David to cover his adultery with Bathsheba. She became pregnant with David's child. But God called David a man after God's own heart. (see Judges 16, 2 Samuel 11)

David raised dysfunctional children. David's son raped his own sister. David did nothing about it. David's other son wanted to take over David's rule as king and tried to kill David but ended up being killed. (see 2 Samuel 13)

Abraham had a habit of lying when he and Sarah were in adverse circumstances. (see Genesis 12, 20)

After God had preserved Noah and his family through the flood, Noah got drunk and his sons found him lying naked in his tent. (see Genesis 9) How disappointing!

God used Rahab, a prostitute to help save the lives of the spies who were sent to spy out the land to determine if the Israelites could capture it. This prostitute is listed in the lineage of Jesus. (see Joshua 2, Matthew 1)

Peter and Paul each exhibited weaknesses in their own ways. Peter had foot-in-mouth disease on numerous occasions. (see Matthew 16, Mark 8, and Luke 4) He denied he even knew Jesus just before Jesus was crucified. (see Matthew 26) Paul was a grandiose, religious, boasting zealot who hated the Christians. (see Acts 9) He had numerous Christians murdered, even witnessing Stephen's stoning. (see Acts 7-8)

Peter sometimes reacted in prejudice and fear. Jews were not supposed to eat with Gentiles, but God had shown Peter that all Christians were clean, and so they could eat together. Peter ate with the new Gentile converts. Later, some prestigious Jewish leaders came to meet with Peter and Paul. Peter immediately moved to another table. (see Acts 11, Galatians 2)

Thomas has been known down through the centuries as Doubting Thomas. He would not believe until he had factual proof that Jesus was indeed alive. (see John 20) How many people do we know who are like Thomas?

In the book of Jonah, we see how God told Jonah to go to Ninevah, and Jonah ran in the opposite direction.

God wants to use our weakness to show His strength. When the Israelites were to fight the Midianites and the Amalekites, God told Gideon to send 32,000 soldiers home. Gideon was allowed to keep just 300 men. God used this tiny group of soldiers to defeat "all the children of the east that lay along in the valley like locusts for multitude; and their camels were without number, as the sand which is upon the seashore." (Judges 7:12) Even today the country of Israel, the size of Connecticut, has the world turned upside down by her tiny existence.

God opposes the prideful but gives grace to the humble (see James 4:6). He uses the very people we would not expect Him to use. He knows our frame; God is mindful that we are but dust (see Psalm 103:14) and uses us anyway. I love the story where God uses a donkey to speak to the prophet Balaam and chastens Balaam for not obeying (see Numbers 22:26). God speaking through a donkey gives each of us much hope, as I realized that if God can use a donkey He can surely use me! How much more foolish can you get than that?

Jesus loved to show God's acceptance of us in our weakness. Jesus said "Blessed are the poor in spirit for theirs is the kingdom of heaven. Blessed are those who mourn for they shall be comforted." (Matthew 5:3-4) Why? Because these people know they are sick, weak, and cannot fix life. Rather than turning away from God they turn toward Him. Jesus also said, "It is not those who are healthy who need a physician, but those who are sick; I did not come to call the righteous, but sinners." (Mark 2:17) He calls and uses those who recognize they are sick and seek His aid.

In the parable of the mustard seed, Jesus points us to the faith God can use to do His will. The mustard seed was the smallest known seed, but when planted, it would become the largest of garden trees where birds and small animals find shelter. Jesus said, "If you have the faith as a mustard seed, nothing will be impossible to you." (see Mark 4:31)

5. **Journal your thoughts about these weak people as to how they relate to you. How do they make you feel?**

## God's Power Alone

Strength in weakness is the theme exemplified in Zechariah 4:6. "This is the word of Jehovah unto Zerubbabel, saying, 'not by might, nor by power, but by my Spirit,' saith the Lord." God desires to work in and through weak vessels to show the world His power. He brings glory and honor to Himself, not only as the King of Kings and Lord of Lords, but also as a loving Father who gives His children His special power. God receives the praise, honor, and thanksgiving from His children as vessels being used. We as vessels benefit because we recognize we are being used mightily of God in spite of our weaknesses. His actions on our behalf strengthen our faith.

As I have indicated in previous chapters, I have never felt strong or capable. It is this fact that continues to encourage me to write this book. I am not an academician, a theologian, an author, or a famous authority. According to God's standards, I have all the qualifications to write this book: nothing but God's calling and His strength.

Each moment I am keenly aware of how the Lord has brought me from insecurity and weakness to His strength in my weakness. My dad tells the story of dropping me off at my high school dance. He recounts how sad he felt watching me stand where he left me on the sidewalk, my little high school beanie on my head (a type of hat that freshmen were to wear) looking lost and scared. I stood there as if frozen. This picture symbolizes who I was on the inside. Over time I learned how to cover up how I felt, but I didn't really change. This was not a godly weakness, but later in my life God used that weakness to bring me to Himself. Today, my life reflects His strength: "But in all these things we overwhelmingly conquer [and gain surpassing victory] through Him who loved us." (Romans 8:37) Godly strength in weakness has hope in God and not in ourselves.

For significant change to take place in our lives, we need not fear our inadequacies. God understands our weaknesses. At first, facing our inadequacies is a disappointing and sad place to find oneself. God ministers to us there and shows us what He can now do through us and for us. Hopefully, we will embrace the truth of our weakness and be finished with judging ourselves. We can find His strength in our weakness.

**6. Do you naturally feel strong and capable, or weak and inadequate? Journal your thoughts about these feelings and how they impact your life.**

### *Where Did It Go?*

When we struggle with an issue and come to the end of our strength, we often want to give up ever being a good Christian. (This is good. Remember, *trying to be good enough* is toxic!) We are without hope. Rather than seeing that *giving up* as good news, far too often we are crestfallen and in despair. Now we are exactly where God wants us. He waits for us to give up trying to be good enough. Instead of despair, we can turn to God to discover what He can do with us.

The temptation will be not to trust God's ability but to trust in some other entity as the change agent. Personal change is not immediate. The period of time it takes for the manifestation of our prayer is what I call *the Weakness with Hope Period.* We are yearning to change our behavior but cannot; however, we hope in our God to do so. One day it is gone. "Where did it go? I'm healed of my weakness. I had nothing to do with it except agree with God it needed to go and trust Him to change me. I did not judge myself while I waited. He changed me. He gets the glory!"

A friend of mine greatly desired to quit smoking. He knew he was not honoring God with his body, which is the temple of the Holy Spirit. After many starts and stops, he finally got sick and tired of being sick and tired and came to that place where he told God, "My smoking is Your problem. We both want it gone. You have got to do it; I cannot do it myself." My friend went on with his life. He would remind himself who had the problem when he was tempted to smoke. "God has the problem." Several months later while driving his car, the sun shown in his face. He pulled down the sun visor. To his surprise into his lap fell a pack of cigarettes! He was flabbergasted as he realized he had not thought about or had a cigarette in over two weeks. God had done it!

7. **Do you have something in your life that you need to give over to God? Journal your thoughts about this struggle, and write about giving it to God.**

## *Contentment*

While Paul says "When I am weak then I am strong," (2 Corinthians 12:10) Paul also says, "I have learned to be content whatever the circumstances." (Philippians 4:11) Weakness and contentment do not seem compatible. When we sense we are not as mature in Christ as we should be, we start yearning to be someplace out there in the future. We are not content. Judging and condemning ourselves comes naturally. Yet it is not *where* we are today that matters, but the fact that we are *going with God* that matters most to Him.

When Moses asked God what to tell the children of Israel when they asked him who had sent him, God gave Moses His name for the first time in history, saying, "I AM that I AM." (Exodus 3) God lives in the present. He is always

I AM every minute of every day. He does not live in the future and neither should we. He does not live in the past and neither should we. You have a relationship with Him at this very moment in time and space. Ask yourself how that relationship is at this moment. If you can say, "It's okay right this moment," then rejoice and stay in the moment. If it is not okay, this is your weakness today. Tell God and give that weakness over to Him to fix.

**8. Do you have contentment today? Journal your thoughts and feelings about contentment.**

# I Give Up!

On first becoming a Christian, I was not aware of the sanctification process we all go through. I somehow thought *now I am free and empowered by the Holy Spirit, so I will be like Jesus.* Of course, I kept running into myself and found myself to be a stumbling block for reaching that goal. I was mad at myself for being so slow.

I attended a workshop entitled, "Do You Have to Give Up Being a Christian in Order to Be Healed of Codependency?" While I was enjoying the small group dynamic, I had a solemn moment of realization. A young pastor asked a rhetorical question that was filled with sadness. "I will never be like Jesus in this lifetime, will I?" I could see the pain in his face as the reality hit him. He so wanted to be able to do everything God required. (Wonderful heart motivation but a toxic ideal to try to reach!) He very much wanted to please Him. At that moment I sensed a tightening in my throat. Tears began to form deep within me. While the young pastor spoke, grieving welled up in my heart. He had just expressed what I was feeling but for which I had no words.

Knowing I could never truly please Jesus with my life was devastating. (Good motivation but a toxic lie to try to reach!) I now know that I please Jesus by just being His Father's child. Another reason I believe I was grieving was the reality that if I could not be like Jesus in this lifetime, I would remain forever in my pain of inadequacy. (a toxic lie) The grieving lasted on and off for three years. Even though toxic lies played into my grieving, I sensed God saying, "Micky your heart is right and I honor that."

A moment of truth came while I was in my therapist's office. I was railing about how I disliked being inadequate. I had always experienced my therapist as compassionate and encouraging. She would listen and validate me. So when I was whining and said with disdain, "I am so inadequate!" I did not expect her response. She replied, "Yes, you are inadequate." Ouch! Where was the empathy? She went on to explain, "We are all inadequate as human beings in light of God's perfection and holiness." I got the message. Being inadequate is reality, *so stop whining, Micky.* Contentment comes to us as a result of embracing God's estimation of ourselves, finding true God Esteem. When I accepted, "Micky, you ARE inadequate," I was empowered to let go of perfectionism and condemnation. Letting go brought a release in my spirits that says, "I no longer have to fight myself, making myself, forcing myself to do God's will. I no longer have to obsess over *shoulds* and *oughts* of life. I no longer have to be a perfectionist, a works-oriented believer, judging and condemning myself for not doing or being enough. I no longer live under the Law but under grace!"

For the person who knows in their heart they cannot perform for God any longer, this becomes very good news. Truth took its place in my heart. I am inadequate and am still loved by God! As I began to face my sadness, God helped me realize He had made provisions to use my weaknesses to glorify Him. I am just to bring those weaknesses to Him for His strength. A relief with hope began as I realized being inadequate can be of benefit in the kingdom of God.

9. **Can you say from your heart of hearts, "I am inadequate, and I am still loved by God"? What does this mean for you?**

## In Summary

When we declare and accept our weaknesses; joy and peace come, knowing we are in agreement with the Lover of our souls. The Good News begins to make sense. Jesus lived the perfect Christian life for us. He took all of our sins (our inability to live the Christian life) onto Himself at the cross so that we might become part of God's family. Now as imperfect, weak children of God we are romping around and enjoying the perfect Father, Son, and Holy Spirit, without the encumbrances of guilt, shame, and self-condemnation.

Dear sister/brother in Christ, there is no shame in coming to the cross over and over again. "It was for freedom that Christ set you free. Keep standing firm and do not subject yourself again to a yoke of slavery." (Galatians 5:1) Boast in your weakness, so the power of God may dwell in you. Rest in the knowledge it is not your own strength "for it is God who all the while is effectually at work in you [energizing and creating in you the power and the desire], both to will and to work for His good pleasure, satisfaction, and delight." (Philippians 2:13)

# CHAPTER 9

# AUTHENTICITY

## *It Means Being Real*

### *The Invitation*

*There He was again! I could make out that silhouette instantly. Up on the hill, He walked along arrayed in splendor! The breeze dancing with His robe gave the appearance that He walked on air. Yet, I leaned out squinting and covering my brow to see each foot actually came to touch the ground. Down the hillside He approached, brightening the dark valley with His presence.*

*Moments later passing my abode, He stopped to extend His scarred hand directly toward me, just out of my reach . . . from the shadows I looked down, fidgeting and mumbling, "I'm okay in here." I glanced up slightly to witness His reaction. His eyes pierced my soul with such compassion that I forced my face back into the shadows. "Do you want to come out and be real with Me?" He asked.*

*I did, but I didn't. It sounded wonderful. But doing it was something else altogether. I had become*

*strangely comfortable in the safety of this little booth
I had grown up in. Cracking the door years ago had
allowed a ray of His light to reach inside. Although
unsightly now under His illumination, these walls
felt somehow safe. They held the shame and loneli-
ness I embraced inside. I did not realize it until that
moment, but these walls had become my friends. I
examined their condition. Funny, I couldn't recall
noticing any odor. Then, I couldn't remember the last
time I had ventured outside of them. I did want to
answer Him, but I could not seem to get the words
out. Finally, they came.*

*"Yes, I do!" I said out loud. But in all of my
hidden pain and insecurity, and that thing I've never
shared with anyone, how could He love me? And how
could I ever trust Him with all this? I wondered. His
beautiful blazing eyes drew my gaze back up where I
found His warm smile still there.*

*"One day you will," He said.*

*By Ashley Wille*

## Authenticity Means Realness

The truths we have discussed thus far are meant to bring
you to this place: authenticity. *Authenticity*, by definition, means being *real*: genuine, sincere, earnest, and with
an absence of pretense. Peter describes Jesus as, "a man who
did not sin, neither was guile [cunning, craftiness, deceit]
found in his mouth" (1 Peter 3:10, author's bracket). Jesus
is authentic. His words and actions are congruent with His
heart. Jesus is exactly who He claims to be: the Son of God.
He is fully trustworthy with a depth of genuine feeling
toward the lost. He outwardly expresses love to those who
know they are sinners in need of help. He speaks His heart in

sadness or anger to those who believe they do not need Him. Through and through, Jesus is real.

Ending the war with yourself brings you freedom to be the person God foresaw before the foundation of the world. Authenticity comes as our shame and our self condemnation and judgment are gone. We accept ourselves for who we are with our weaknesses and where we are in our Sanctification Program. We welcome God's directives because it is not all up to us to do in our strength. This inner journey we go through is the foundation of revival. If not a church wide revival or nationwide revival, then it is a personal revival. Personal revival and authenticity merge together to free us from our false selves.

Personal revival and corporate revival is blocked by inauthenticity, because the essence of revival is people willing to be emotionally open, honest, and authentic: real with others and with God. When we end the war with ourselves we are free to come out of hiding. When our shame is gone our personal revival is contagious. The world is desperately looking for authentic believers, who are relevant to a hurting world.

Authentic Christians are not only eager to grow in the Lord, but welcome insight into how they are missing God's will. They desire God to reveal to them those things that displease Him and then choose to grow in any situation life throws at them. Christians who are authentic understand that sharing their strengths, weaknesses, and struggles will help others who are struggling.

The question now at hand is *how open and real can you be with the members of your local body of Christ?* Are you free to reveal you struggles, you pain, you sins, your doubts? Can you be the church to the church? It is curious how seldom I hear someone ask for prayer for themselves. Prayer generally is for Aunt Susan, the neighbor down the street, the child in the hospital. There is a fear of being real with the very people who should be emotionally safe for us.

1. **How authentic (real) are you with others? How authentic are you with your friends at church? Can you talk about how you really feel and who you really are?**

## Integrity

We also see integrity in Jesus. Integrity denotes oneness of character, being the same inside and outside. To be a person of integrity one must exhibit truthfulness, honor, reliability, honesty, and authenticity. People of integrity do not play games with others or manipulate them. If they need something, they ask directly without hidden agendas. Their agendas are brought out into the open. Everything is on the table.

As we end the war with ourselves, others begin to experience us as people of integrity. Let's use Joe as an example of a Christian who is authentic and a person of integrity. Let's say he is your boss. You watch him carefully because you've heard he was one of those born-again Christians. When you notice him make a mistake you find him admitting his mistake. When the team is taken in a direction it should not have gone, he takes ownership and apologizes openly in the staff meeting. You notice a team member comes up with a great idea and it is successfully implemented. You see your boss give all the credit that is due to that team member. Later, you discover when he meets with the senior officers of the company, rather than taking the praise himself, he once again gives credit to your team member.

When your boss says he will do something, you know he will follow through. John has no ulterior motives other than to show himself approved by God and to help his fellow workers be the best they can be, based on their talents and skills. He has no intention of promoting himself. He will allow God to promote him in due time. He lives in the moment, enjoying the moment and leaving the future to God.

**2. What does integrity mean for you? How do you live with integrity?**

# Deception

The flipside of authenticity is deception. The Pharisees were deceivers. They pretended to be spiritual but in truth were inauthentic. We recognize them as hypocrites. Jesus had a lot to say about people like the Pharisees who are not authentic: "In the same way, on the outside you appear to people as righteous but on the inside you are full of hypocrisy and wickedness... You snakes! You brood of vipers! How will you escape being condemned to hell?" (Matthew 23:28, 33) What indignation Jesus felt for hypocrisy! The ultimate father of deception is Satan, "That ancient serpent who is called the devil and Satan, the deceiver of the whole world." (Revelation 12:9)

If we were to take a modern-day example of hypocrisy and follow it to its final conclusion, we would understand how evil hypocrisy really is and the damage it does to others. My pastor has shed tears over his own hypocrisy. He was ordained in a liturgical denomination that was more interested in the correct vestments for the season of the year and where you stood during communion, than in a relationship with God. Several times he was called on the carpet for standing in the wrong place during the service or wearing the wrong vestments. Little discussion or help focused on his faith and his walk with the Lord. Yet he played this game for years. His tears, he said, were for the people he should have been ministering to rather than worrying about ecclesiastical traditions. He now leads a large non-denominational, non-liturgical church, where he can minister to people with authenticity, focusing on real faith and walking with the Lord.

3. **Recall a time when you were deceived or you deceived someone. Journal the impact on you or the other person.**

## Why So Many Hypocrites?

Churches and parents often inadvertently depict the Christian life as a program for living, primarily based on rules of behavior. Members do not experience the church as emotionally safe. Learning what the Bible says seems to be the main focus in evangelical churches. Our internal lives are rarely given attention. Fear can motivate the Christian to keep to acceptable behavior by following the rules.

When we focus only on following the rules, we are unknowingly training our children to become hypocrites instead of true believers. Donald Sloat, a Christian psychologist, contends, "When fear is the motivating force behind our behavior, we engage in avoidance behavior. Avoidance behaviors are not deeply personal or from the heart, but are superficial, defensive actions to guard against criticism or rejection. These reactions are developed in response to the threat, and so do not promote personal growth or integration" of God's Word into their hearts.

Ego defenses and denial can also cause hypocrisy within the church. We delude ourselves with ego defenses that serve to shield ourselves from negative truth. We want to escape judgment and retain our positive self esteem. Often we do this by comparing ourselves with others who may be weaker in a certain area than we are. In this way, we can delude ourselves into thinking we are good enough as we are. Denial is self-delusion. We deny there is anything wrong. "Sin? I'm not a sinner! Dysfunctional? Oh, maybe a little. Imperfect? No one is perfect! But all and all, compared to others, I'm a pretty nice person." God Esteem is very different from this self delusion.

Another reason Christians are not authentic is church leaders, pastors, Sunday school teachers, deacons, and associate pastors do not lead with authenticity before the people they are leading. I am not saying they should reveal everything negative that is going on in their lives, but they can be honest about having their own struggles as my pastor did regarding his sadness at having been a hypocrite. When leaders will admit to no struggle, they cannot show how God has worked with them. They can hold the congregation back from authenticity, by leaving them without an example. Sheep naturally go only as far as their shepherd can lead. The church at large helps perpetuate being inauthentic by not addressing the issue. Our churches need to provide a format, a safe place, for members to speak up about their sins, their wounds, their struggles, and about any questions they may have.

I was once part of a church where it was not the norm to be authentic. We were a smiling church. Members backed away in droves if someone did break the norm and say they had serious problems. I believe they back away because they have little experience with authenticity and do not know how to handle the honesty of another person. Inauthenticity is a breeding ground for hypocrisy. Like our leaders, I was afraid to speak up and be authentic. I convinced myself and can still convince myself that I am a pretty nice sinner. I tried and succeeded to externally measure up to what a nice sinner might be. "I am not a part of the society's problem. I follow the rules. I am kind to people." I learned early on that if I smiled and was pleasant, people liked me, but under the smile and the niceness, no one seemed to be home.

I occasionally visited a church where people are encouraged to be open and honest. I once invited a friend from my previous church to go to this church one Sunday. On our way there, she said, "I told my husband this morning, 'I sure am glad I am going to a church today where at least they know they are sick!'" Jesus came for the sick, but too often we actually enable people to cover up and help perpetuate their sicknesses. We need to practice being authentic, rather than being hypocrites.

4. **Think about the last time you were at your church. Did you engage in a conversation with authenticity? Journal your thoughts about what being authentic within the church means for you.**

## Impression Management

For a long time impression management ruled my life. I married a young, aspiring attorney. I had two adorable little blond-headed blue-eyed boys. We were able to build a house in an old Atlanta neighborhood. I had just been asked to join a prestigious woman's organization. And to top it off, my children were in *the* private school. I easily gave the impression that I was living the American dream. But I was miserable. My husband and I fought constantly. He had come from a broken home, and his relational skills seemed broken. I was an only child who never baby sat and had absolutely no parenting skills. Each day was another day of survival, trying to maintain the impression of the perfect American family. This would cost my integrity, and the emotional well-being of my children and husband. I was on a treadmill going nowhere.

After putting up the last chandelier and volunteering my new house for numerous ladies' functions, the excitement of having a new home began to wane. My younger son was diagnosed with learning disabilities, so we had to move him from the private school to one that could help him. I am sorry to admit I felt shame. I began to feel out of place rubbing elbows with the ladies in the club I had joined. What was going on inside of me was nothing like the impression I worked to maintain. I had all the right notches on my belt to be accepted. I was stuck.

I felt like the Wizard, in the Wizard of Oz. Do you remember how the Wizard amazed and frightened everyone in the Land of Oz? Dorothy, the Tin Man, the Lion, Scarecrow and Toto, the dog, came to the Wizard to ask him to send Dorothy back to her home, for a heart for the Tin Man, courage for the Lion, and a brain for the Scarecrow. The Wizard spoke with a thunderous, condescending voice. As they cowered before the Wizard's curtain, Toto, unbeknownst to the others, grabbed the curtain in his teeth and pulled it open. Lo and behold, the Wizard was exposed. Who was he? He was a tiny little man speaking through a megaphone hidden behind a curtain. The Wizard had held the citizens of Oz captive with fear for many years. All the while, he was just as frightened as they were. I identified with the frightened and trembling little man behind the curtain. Because I had no idea of who I really was, I hid behind the curtain to emotionally and socially survive. I even tried on other people's personalities to see if any fit. I felt like a chameleon, trying on other people's personalities to find one that would please other people.

Then I came to know the Lord! God began my inner journey to authenticity, and I began to find relief. I did not completely understand all the ramifications of receiving Him as my Savior. I knew nothing of authenticity, just impression management. I did not know how to be real. I listened to other people's prayer requests. They never asked prayer for themselves. I concluded they must not have problems like I had. So I was quiet. If I really told people what was going on inside of me and asked for prayer, I thought they would be shocked and not want to be my friend.

Years later I discovered how many in these groups were feeling the same way I had felt. They too believed that the others were not having problems and that was why they were not asking for prayer for themselves. I realize now I missed so many opportunities to help others. By sharing my story of frailty, I could have authentically connected with them, and may have led them to share their struggles and fears with me. This is how the body of Christ is supposed to work!

5. **How do you engage in impression management? What do you fear about being authentic?**

## Rick's Story

Authenticity involves being the same person in private that we are in public and being the same person in public that we are in private. Our culture today sees political correctness as bringing private selves out of the closet with little to no thought of becoming anything else. We are not to let our sin nature run rampant, but to reveal our hearts and our desire for God to heal us. Rick's story shares a path to authenticity for our learning.

Rick knew the Bible and taught a Sunday school class, so others saw him as a strong Christian. But he was privately addicted to pornography. When he was ten years old, he found magazines in his father's trunk in the basement, and he would sneak down to look at them. He got hooked. As an adult he was spending thousands of dollars a year on his addiction. With internet access, he no longer had to go to sleazy stores, but could find and buy whatever fed this hunger in the comfort and secrecy of his own home. Rick knew his actions did not line up with the impression he gave at church. Because he was a Christian, his soul was terribly conflicted. He knew he was a hypocrite as he kept his secret. Rick was not authentic. He was not what psychology calls *congruent* with himself or with others. Rick had only two choices: to continue to hide his addiction, or to confess it. Both would have diametrically opposite outcomes.

### *Hiding His Addiction*

Rick thought he had completely hidden his addiction, but his ten-year-old son had discovered his father's pornography. One afternoon the child's mother caught her son and realized these were Rick's websites. She was devastated. She confronted Rick, but he chose denial: he said their son must have accidentally come across this on the internet. She doubted her husband's answer, and trust between them began to erode.

Trust is the foundation of a healthy relationship. Trust or mistrust is the first thing a child learns about the world. If trust is there, the child develops a healthy sense of connectedness with others both now and for the future. If trust is broken, the roads are many that lead to impaired painful relationships. When trust is gone, we have absolutely nothing to rest a relationship on. So what happened to Rick?

Rick's wife continued to find more and more evidence. Determined not to enable his evil habit, she moved out of the house, taking their son. Rick was devastated and wanted them back, but continued on with the pornography. Finally, she divorced him. When the church discovered why she divorced Jack, people were devastated. "How could he? He is such a godly man!"

Sin always reaps bad consequences, and habitual sin deepens painful consequences. Rick opened Pandora's Box by not acknowledging his sin to himself, to God and to someone safe. If Rick does not get help, many different scenarios could follow. What outcome will his son and his wife have? In one scenario, the son will follow in his father's footsteps like Rick did. In another scenario, his wife might be so wounded she will never trust another man. Rick may begin acting out his sexual perversions, as Ted Bundy did. Bundy kidnapped college students, raped them, and then killed them. Before he died, Bundy credited the murders to pornography, which led to snuff films. Snuff films show a perpetrator who rapes and really kills the victim on film. Who knows the final outcome of Rick's life? When we cross God's boundaries, we open Pandora's Box, and our lonely lives fill with horrible conflict.

7.  **Do you know someone who is a Christian who was exposed for a concealed sin? How did finding out about this impact you? How do you explain this phenomenon in a Christian's life?**

### *Confessing His Sin to a Christian in Authority*

How can sinners (like Rick and like me and you) be authentic when we know we cannot be perfect? Our lives should match our theology. What we believe about God should match with how we act: this is integrity. Christians need integrity to recognize to God, self, and others the areas in their lives that do not match with the Word of God. When we recognize this lack of integrity, we can find healing. Healing for Rick would begin by confessing his addiction to someone in authority within the Christian community and seeking help, prayer and accountability with that person. Rick might confess his sin to his Sunday school teacher, a church leader, or some other person he sees is dedicated to authenticity. He would then find integrity by being who he says he is, a person who loves the Lord but is trapped in pornography and desires healing and deliverance from this addiction. God has redeemed Rick, and He redeems the struggle Rick will have to reach wholeness. Rick's life can be used more powerfully than ever in God's kingdom as people will be drawn to his authenticity in Christ.

Is it imperative to actually tell someone about the sin? We ask God's forgiveness. God tells us "if we confess to one another our faults, our slips, our false steps, our offenses, our sins; and pray for one another, we will be healed and restored to a spiritual tone of mind and heart." (James 5:16a). We must come out of our prayer closets and use one of the greatest resources God has given us for healing: the body of Christ. Just as telling someone you have received Christ's gift of grace is confessing your salvation, (Romans 10:10) confessing our sins to one another makes real our commitment to God's healing. It takes humility to speak out about our sin, but we find grace in humbling ourselves. "For God sets Himself against the *proud* [the insolent, the overbearing, the disdainful, the presumptuous, the boastful He opposes, frustrates, and defeats], but gives grace [favor, blessing] to the *humble*." (1 Peter 5:5)

**8. Is there sin you have been hiding? Journal about this, and confess it to God. Do you have a Christian with whom you can share? Why is this important?**

## The Body of Christ: a Community of Authenticity

The body of Christ has been created by God, not only for Himself but for us, too. The individual members of the body of Christ are to support, encourage, hold accountable, discipline, teach, and worship together. The body of Christ is to be a resource of comfort and a refuge of safety for us. Within the context of the church God calls us to share with one another our struggles and sin.

We can share our burdens within the Body of Christ as a safe and confidential environment where true healing manifests itself. Harper's Bible Dictionary defines *burden* as "a heavy load, creating psychological and spiritual anxiety." We must be willing to stop covering up what we know to be detrimental to others and ourselves. We may be tempted to protect ourselves from talking about humbling or embarrassing life truths, but protecting ourselves is not really protecting ourselves at all. It is ultimately harmful to us and our relationships. When we are willing to share *our issues* with another, it shows we are serious about being authentic with God, ourselves, and others. God sees and honors our hearts.

As we become more authentic, we may appear to others to be backsliding. The person learning to honor the uniqueness of who they are in Christ may be led to drop involvement in certain activities as they discover these activities are not God's best for them. They learn to deny requests that do not reflect who they are called to be. Some church members may think authentic people are less mature and their lives are less inviting than people who manage their impressions, but who are caught in denial and co-dependency. Actually, the reverse is true: as we become more mature, we are more likely to recognize the ache in another's soul and be able to minister to them out of our brokenness and God's healing.

**9. With whom do you share your burdens? What is it like for you to share your burdens with another person?**

### *Building a Confessional Church Community*

How may we help others become authentic in Christian group settings? Carl Rogers described becoming authentic as "a process by which the individual drops one after another of the defensive masks with which he has faced life, so that he may experience fully the hidden aspects of himself."

We may begin building a Christian confessional community within the church we attend, or if necessary, outside the church. We think of Christian community as covered dish dinners or a Sunday School Christmas party or Wednesday night suppers. These are programs designed to build community, but may be a superficial way of knowing and ministering to others. At these events, we often share only facts about ourselves, such as, "My name is Sam. I am in marketing. I've been a member here for five years. My wife and I have three children."

Sunday schools, Bible studies, and church services are another part of building community. We must set apart Christ as Lord, and be ready to give an answer for our hope. (1 Peter 3:15) Too often, these meetings teach us the Bible as intellectual facts, without authentic community with the people around us. Small, confidential groups can be an expedient way to develop authenticity within a church. God not only can change us individually through true community, but can change the church and its reputation from hypocrisy to authenticity.

True community is created when believers are transparent and confessional with each other. The members of an authentic community have permission to self-disclose, confess, and ask for prayer for the painful issues in their lives. The group learns not to judge, or try to fix the other person with advice. They learn to keep confidentiality. They share their real selves and pray for each other; they give encouragement, accountability, and acceptance to each other. In this safe environment, they truly learn how to humble themselves before God and before others by being confessional. In this environment of humility and owning their own particular sickness, God works mightily in His children.

## 10. Are you part of an authentic Christian community? Journal what it would be like for you to be part of an authentic Christian community.

### *Sharing Your Struggles*

Because God loves us, we don't have to be ashamed anymore. Once our shame is gone we can be authentic, free to share our frailties and struggles and the grace, power, and acceptance Jesus gives us. I believe a revival would start if we were authentic with Christians and non-Christians alike. The non-believer would take us seriously if we would humbly admit we are not what we desire to be, but still God really loves us!

A research study entitled "Effects of Reciprocity and Self-monitoring on Self-Disclosure with a New Acquaintance" (by S.M. Jourard) suggests how to help the church become more authentic. The study asserts that a subject's level of self-disclosure is matched by a partner's level of self-disclosure; this has been repeatedly demonstrated in laboratory experiments. This phenomenon, called *disclosure reciprocity*, means that if a person self-discloses, then the other person will self-disclose at the same level as their friend. If one person stays on the surface, so will the other. If one person shares some current struggle they are experiencing, so will the other.

I propose that pastors, Sunday school teachers, deacons, parents, teens, counselors, members and Bible study teachers take the initiative to be transparent and self-disclose. As we do so, the principle of disclosure reciprocity will free others to begin sharing their innermost pain and confusion. As they are accepted and not rejected by us, fragile people will begin to open themselves to the ministry of the Holy Spirit and growth toward healing will begin. As individuals within a church become authentic and this spreads to others within the church, in this multiplication, we will begin a revival!

The end goal of self-disclosure is not just for transparency. As we authentically express where we are, we must continue to look to our God of grace and be reminded that He is not surprised by the inner emotional pain and suffering we may express to Him. As David Seamonds, in his book *Healing of Damaged Emotions* so eloquently reminds us, "Grace is never shocked, never repulsed, and never withdrawn, whatever it is faced with. It is freely given, without any references to our goodness or badness, worthiness or unworthiness."

**11. Journal about a time when you authentically shared yourself with another. What was that experience like? Did you experience grace or condemnation? How did this make you feel? Did you go together to God for help and healing?**

## *My Church and Yours*

Several years ago my church began a program to bring together wounded members for seeking God's healing in their lives. No one could imagine how well this program would be accepted and attended. We now have two different programs, with an informal follow up group; a short introductory program, and a 26 week program.

Twice a year we have an introductory, eight-week program. As an open group, you can come once, try it out and decide if you want to come back. You can also join the group after it has begun meeting. The meeting consists of singing praise and worship; teaching that integrates teaching biblical principles and human psychological concepts; an experiential activity for the group; and small group interaction for the purpose of being confessional and sharing prayer for God to heal inner wounds.

Our twenty-six week, long program is a closed meeting structure; fees are paid as a commitment to participating, as well as to fund study books, a Christmas Dinner and an Ending Celebration Dinner. The format is the same as the introductory program, with the addition of weekly home-work which is completed and turned in to each individual's small group leader. Two small group leaders have a group of just four or five participants.

Critical mass is building in our church. We have an unusu-ally open congregation. One of our resent Congregational Care Pastors said, "Within the short period of time I have been here I have seen more people with serious problems come to me for help than in all my years of pastoral care." You may think, "You must have a lot of sick people at your church." Remember Jesus came for the sick, and we are coming to Him to be healed. Program participants sometimes repeat participa-tion two or three times. They are intent on accepting God's grace for their sin, and internalizing the love of God to heal their wounds.

**12. How is or is not your church a place of authenticity? Journal how you feel about this.**

## The Growing Result

We have seen some miraculous changes and some subtle changes in the people who go through our programs. Some who have gone through the program are now turning back around to help others as leaders for future programs. Talking about this ministry, one member of the church said, "We are doing church here. This is what a church is supposed to be." The rich experience of open sharing and authenticity in the program causes many participants to hesitate joining a regular Bible Study or Sunday school class. To our delight, we have seen some bring authenticity to these classes and positively influence others to be more authentic, too.

Churches often don't know what to do with people struggling with brokenness and wounds. I believe these very people are potential leaders: as they have willingly participated with God in their healing and are confessional with others in that process, they can understand another's pain. Jesus shows us His example as "He saw a great crowd waiting, and He was moved with compassion for them, because they were like sheep without a shepherd." (Mark 6:34a) An authentic Christian is moved with compassion because they experienced Jesus' compassion for them; they have learned to treat themselves with His compassion, so they can share His compassion with others.

(For further information contact http://www.desert-stream.org)

**13. How have you experienced Jesus' compassion for you? How do you share His compassion with others?**

# In Summary

God and the unbelieving world, along with our significant others, cry out for Christians to be authentic, people of integrity. It is only when we are real that an unbelieving world will feel safe enough to listen to us. We can share only as much as we have received from Jesus. Authenticity is about being honest with ourselves, with God, and with others regarding our struggles, sins, and wounds. It is about sharing with others, that in spite of ourselves, we are loved and accepted by God. It is about allowing God to renew our minds in order to experientially actualize who we truly are in Christ.

Authentic Christians are certainly not perfect in their walk with the Lord. They choose God Esteem instead of the world's self esteem. They focus on authentically living to please God. Living authentically creates satisfying relationships for all involved. We learn to walk with God in the assurance that we cannot live by hiding our shame. Our academic Biblical knowledge becomes heart knowledge of the Truth. We stop attacking ourselves with our negative slams. We are authentic when we say about ourselves what God says about us. With Paul, our hearts sing, "There is therefore now no condemnation [for me] because I am in Christ Jesus!" (Romans 8:1) Amen.

# CHAPTER 10

# RESTING IN GOD'S SABBATH REST

## *As Close to Home As We Can Be*

### *Running Out of Yourself*

*I picked up my friend for lunch early one after-noon. In an earlier phone call, we had begun a discus-sion about Sabbath rest; now we enjoyed continuing our conversation. My car was new, in good condition and relatively comfortable to ride in, or so I thought. Slowing down to inch along in midday traffic, we came to a halt in the sea of cars. Suddenly, my friend jumped out and disappeared behind my car.*

*Where was she going? Baffled by her behavior, I tried to stay calm as horns blasted and traffic began to roll. I found her in my rearview mirror: she was trying to push my car! I lowered my window and yelled, "Have you lost your mind? Get in the car!" "You should be back here helping me!!" she retorted.*

*I rolled into a parking lot. Glaring at me, she blasted me with a long tirade on work ethic, duty, and laziness. "So let me get this straight," I said. "You sincerely believe my V6 engine needs your help to move the car down the street? You think we are presumptuous to sit inside while it does all the work?" "Yes! Don't ask me to get back in that car!" she demanded. A mule would have been less stubborn. I tried another explanation and encouraging words, but she still refused to get in the car. I couldn't believe it when she insisted on walking home; it was quite a distance, even for a mule.*

*I will never forget seeing her in my rearview mirror as I pulled out of the parking lot alone. She proudly marched off with her arms firmly folded and her face raised and scowling. I wondered what would bring her to finally run out of herself.*

*By Ashley Wille*

## Resting in Grace

The grand finale of ending the war with yourself is finding God's Sabbath rest. We begin to enter this rest when we learn to esteem ourselves as God does. We know what living under the Law means, and we choose to move back to live in God's grace. We internalize God's grace and love in our hearts so we live, love, and desire to obey God. We choose to enter into this rest and refrain from judgment of ourselves as God has forgiven us. We find our true identity, seeing ourselves as Jesus sees us, instead of the world's estimation of us. When we feel weak to do God's will, we rest in His strength. This is God Esteem in action. We have ended the war with ourselves and are liberated and free to enter

God's rest. In Hebrews 3 and 4, we learn of this Sabbath rest prepared by God for us, His children.

### *Grasshoppers or Landowners*

Hebrews 3 recounts the story of God's desire to provide a place of rest for the children of Israel. He led them out of bondage in Egypt and promised them a land of their own. This Promised Land was a reality awaiting them. But in their unbelief, a lack of trust in God's promise, they would not enter in (Hebrews 3:19). They confessed, "We are but grasshoppers in our own sight and so are we in their sight" (Numbers 13:33). Because of their unbelief, God declared they would wander in the desert for forty years, until all those over twenty years old had died.

God allowed the children of Israel to have their will and suffer their own consequences. They had two choices: enter the land or not. Fearing the inhabitants of the land more than trusting God, they chose not to enter the land. God forces no one to do or be what He desires. As a consequence for their choice, they wandered in the wilderness for forty years. It should have taken them three months to travel from Egypt into the Promised Land. This generation never experienced God's gift of the Promised Land.

Was God angry? Oh yes, he was quite angry. A loving parent would be angry! As a loving parent, you may have bought your sixteen year old a car for his birthday. He seemed disappointed that the car is not up to his standards, but he did drive it. How do you feel when he gets a ticket for DUI? You may have been frustrated that he was disappointed with the car you chose, but you are angry about the DUI. He broke family rules, broke the law, and will suffer the consequences. He will go to court, and you will take the car away from him for a time. Who caused all this trouble – the parent who disciplines, or the son who makes these choices? Obviously, the son has caused his own pain by his actions.

God works with us very much as the parent disciplines the son. When we read stories such as the Israelites wandering in the desert, we feel God's anger, and we may consciously or subconsciously determine He is not safe. At any moment He might unleash His rage on us and like a person wielding a fly swatter at a picnic; splat, we are toast. Instead, we need to see God through the eyes of Jesus, so that we can experience Him as a caring Father who may be outraged at His children's attitudes, actions or inactions; but still continues loving them even as He disciplines them.

**1. Do you ever feel like a grasshopper? When you feel like a grasshopper, what do you think God feels about you? Why?**

### God Promises Rest

As I considered the concept of a Sabbath rest, I wondered: *Is there such rest for us today?* We are invited into His promised rest. (Hebrews 4:1-11) Paul exhorts us four times not to miss entering into God's rest like the children of Israel did. He wants us to know there is a Sabbath rest awaiting us today. Take a few moments to read and consider what Paul says:

> *[1]Therefore, let us fear if, while a promise remains of entering His rest, any one of us may seem to have come short of it. The promise of entering God's rest still stands today. This rest was actualized by His Son, Jesus, who would make a way for us to enter into His Father's rest.*
> *[2]For indeed we have had the glad tidings [Gospel of God] proclaimed to us just as truly as they[the*

*Israelites of old did when the good news of deliver-
ance from bondage came to them]; but the message
they heard did not benefit them, because it was not
mixed with faith [with the leaning of the entire personality on God in absolute trust and confidence in His
power, wisdom, and goodness] by those who heard
it; neither were they united in faith with the ones
[Joshua and Caleb] who heard [and did believe].
The Jews heard the invitation but did not trust God's
wisdom and goodness; no one entered into the
Promised Land except for Joshua and Caleb.*

*³For we who have believed [adhered to and
trusted in and relied on God] do enter that rest, in
accordance with His declaration that those [who did
not believe] should not enter when He said, "As I
swore in My wrath, They shall not enter My rest;"
and this He said although [His] works had been
completed and prepared [and waiting for all who
would believe] from the foundation of the world.
(Hebrews 4:1-3)*

Paul compares us with the children of Israel. We have both
been offered good news of deliverance from bondage. The
children of Israel were offered a promised land and deliverance from the bondage of 400 years in Egypt as slaves. We, on
the other hand, are offered a spiritual and emotional Sabbath
rest from our bondage to sin and condemnation. Like the
children of Israel, many believers still live in bondage even
after trusting Jesus for their eternity. We have two choices.
We can remain in bondage or accept God's invitation to enter
into His rest. "For in a certain place He has said this about
the seventh day: And God rested on the seventh day from
all His works." (Hebrews 4:4) As God rested we are invited
to rest from our good works. "For he who has once entered
[God's] rest also has ceased from [the weariness and pain]

of human labors, just as God rested from those labors peculiarly His own." (Hebrews 4:10)

In his *Commentary on the Whole Bible,* Matthew Henry states, "Every true believer has ceased from his own works of righteousness, and from the burdensome works of the law, as God and Christ have ceased from their works of creation and redemption." We are to rest in Christ's ability through the power of the Holy Spirit within us. With the hymn writer, we can say, "It is well with my soul."

This rest does not mean taking a seat and waiting for life to happen. "Let us therefore be zealous and exert ourselves and strive diligently to enter that rest [of God, to know and experience it for ourselves], that no one may fall or perish by the same kind of unbelief and disobedience [into which those in the wilderness fell]." (Hebrews 4:11) The rest God promises is a rest-as-you-are-going rest. As we go about being mothers, fathers, wives, teens, business people, preachers, or artists, our souls can rest in God's care, giving us God's peace.

We also choose to find freedom from bondage. Jesus often asked, "Do you want to be healed?" He was asking them to declare their will. Many Christians do not experience rest. They are Christians, but they miss God's heart desire for them. They live in frustration, pain, sadness, disconnection, anger; sensing something is wrong in their walk with the Lord. It breaks my heart to find people stuck in their suffering when I know there is a way out for them. They need ears to hear what Jesus would say to them, and will to choose to follow Him to enter His rest.

**2. Journal your thoughts about what it means for you to enter God's rest.**

## Anxiety, Fear, and Pride

Just like the children of Israel, too often we are like grass-hoppers in our own sight. Instead of rest, we are filled with anxiety. Anxiety is fear of the future: fear of things that have not yet happened, but could happen. Much mental energy goes into anxiety, depleting our emotional, physiological and spiritual strength for living. We fret and worry about things out of our control. We are not in control, and we feel powerless to handle certain situations in our lives. Yet, the more we try to control our circumstances, the more anxious we become.

Anxiety and fear are twins. If I fear snakes, when I go into the woods, anxiety will consume me as I fear I may see a snake. If I am truly terrified of snakes, I will not even venture into the woods. My fear has controlled and limited me. God has given us fear, for fear alerts us and drives us to avoid danger. I should avoid poisonous snakes if I don't want to be bitten, but this is not the same as being anxious that a snake will come out of the woods and bite me. Fear that becomes disproportionate to the circumstance at hand impacts the way we make decisions and live our lives. Fear out of control becomes constant anxiety, causing us to make choices that limit and inconvenience ourselves and others.

For years, I lived with anxiety without even recognizing it. You may ask how this could be. Looking back, I think my parents were emotionally unaware, and we never talked about emotions. They couldn't help me understand my emotions. At thirty-one years old, I learned the name for emotions that had gripped me for almost twenty years. A friend asked me for a glass of water so she could take a pill. I asked her, "What is the pill for?" She replied, "For my anxiety." To make conversation, I asked, "What is anxiety like?" She described anxiety: her stomach twisted in knots, her heart pounded, fear rose up in her chest, and thoughts of imminent calamity raced through her head.

Suddenly, I knew anxiety had haunted me from the time I was twelve years old. I constantly suffered stomach problems. The anxiety would keep me awake at night, playing over and over in my head a conversation or a reaction I had that day; always second-guessing myself. I worried about my marriage, my children, and my everyday activities. I did not see my fear or my lack of trust. My learned helplessness increased my fear and my low self esteem intensified my lack of trust in my choices, filling me with anxiety each day.

For years, I tried to control my family so that we would be safe. I was terrified of the teen years as I did not want my children to be hurt physically, mentally, emotionally, or spiritually. Fear would easily override reason, self-control would vanish, and the way I would act and react was quickly outside the fruit of the Spirit. I didn't understand the Spirit was using these circumstances to say to me, "You are not trusting God. Your wounds need healing." Like the children of Israel, I was spinning my wheels, driving far away from the goals I had for my family. I had no peace; life was torture. In such pain, I called and went to a Christian therapist.

I began to see the dynamic of my anxiety. When I was first married, I was perplexed because the people I thought I was trying to help didn't want my help. I began to realize they probably felt pushed, smothered, invalidated, and controlled, but not helped. In reality, I needed control, believing that controlling my circumstances would make my anxiety go away. This runs contrary to the Inside Out principle and ultimately backfired.

3. **Are fear and anxiety a strong dynamic in your life? Journal your thoughts and feelings about your anxiety and fears. Why do you think the anxiety and fears have not been removed from your life?**

## *Looking Inside Anxiety*

Anxiety is a symptom with a cause: we must look inside our anxiety to see its cause. If the children of Israel were our friends, how might we pray for them? We could say, "They are being disobedient. We need to pray about their disobedience." Disobedience is outward behavior; however, inside us are causes for outward behavior. Rather than judging behavior, our compassion for a friend would draw us to look inside this disobedience to find its real cause.

When the children of Israel called themselves grasshoppers, we can feel their fear. Instead of trusting God to bring them into the land, their fear overflows. We can feel their anxiety as they wept, they grumbled, and they whined they would have been better off to have stayed in Egypt than to die in the desert! (see Numbers 13) If you remember that they were slaves in Egypt, you will agree with me that their fear was out of control.

This next point is tricky. When a person feels out of control they tenaciously grab control. A controlling person (on the outside) is really one who feels out of control (on the inside). So when the children of Israel were out of control they became controlling. Collectively, they began to direct the course of their next forty years. God says, "Go!" and they say, "No!" Remember the boundaries God sets for Himself? Since they choose their own control, God allows them to have that control.

A sin of greater consequence than the anxiety, the fear, the control, the lack of trust, and the disobedience is that they do not turn to God and cry out, "We need help! We do not trust You. We are terrified! We are grasping for control. Telling us to go and take the land is like telling a drowning person to swim to shore. Forgive us, God, and help our unbelief." If they had cried out to God in this way, I think the story would have ended differently. God is not concerned that we sometimes feel fear. But fear inside can drive us to call on Him, or to act in disobedience. He can change our hearts, so that we can choose to obey Him in our actions.

The sin that often stands in the way of crying out to God is pride. We seem to think that *we have to save face.* When our pride is strong, our will follows suite. We find it excruciating to admit we are wrong or need help. It is safe to say the children of Israel were in bondage to their pride, spinning their wheels in the desert for forty years. Because they would not be confessional, admitting and owning their fear, God had nothing to work with. Of all the sins, pride is considered the number one stumbling block to spiritual and emotional healing. Who chose the wilderness experience for the children of Israel? God gave them one year in the desert for every day they had explored the land; but the children of Israel chose the wilderness by refusing to enter the land. God may give us consequences, but we are the ones who choose when in fear, anxiety, and pride, not to go to Him.

**4. Journal your thoughts about a time when pride caused you pain.**

## Sabotaging Myself

We have considered how the children of Israel sabotaged their opportunity for living in the Promised Land and how we sabotage our opportunities to trust God and obey Him. As we hear God's promises and respond in faith, we find His rest. We gain further insight from the Bible Reader's Companion: "The concept of God's *rest* is rooted in Creation and has vital meaning for us in our *today* (vv. 4–8). When the Old Testament says God 'rested from His work' it doesn't mean God is inactive. It means God no longer works; that in His act of Creation He planned for every contingency. There is no problem we can face that God has not already provided a solution. Our task then is not to find our own answers. It is to listen for His voice, and be sure He will lead us into His rest (vv. 9–11)."

God has worked out every contingency for our lives prior to His creation of the world and then rested. There is absolutely nothing that can surprise God. He has every possibility covered. In fact, all of God's gifts and the Sabbath rest have been prearranged for us. All this should encourage us to will to pursue this promised rest.

In Romans 8:26-39 we see some of God's immutable provisions for us:

- *The Spirit helps our weaknesses and even prays when we don't know how to pray.*
- *God takes all the garbage of the world thrown at us and turns it for our good. He is committed to forming us into the image of His Son.*
- *He has not only called us to be His child, but also justified us and glorified us.*
- *No one can bring charges against us if God is for us!*
- *God justified us. Jesus will not condemn us. He died for us and makes intercession for us now in heaven.*
- *In the light of these truths, I am convinced nothing can separate us from God's love in Christ Jesus our Lord, so I don't need to fear:*
    - o *High or low things*
    - o *Angels or any other created thing*
    - o *Principalities or powers*
    - o *Present things or future things*
    - o *Life or death*

In a training program, the trainer asked, "What is it that you fear the most?" I heard people saying, "I fear flying." Another said, "I fear standing up in front of people and speaking." On my turn I heard myself say, "I fear myself the most." *Why? Because I know what a mess I can make of things, I need to trust the One who can fix the mess.*

So many forces coming against us, tempting us to doubt—prayers not yet answered, pressures from an out-of-control society, media mania, dire circumstances, our negative self-talk, our own flesh and wounds. Each of us knows that in the blink of an eye we can put ourselves back under the law and experience emotional conflict within. Our pride can even keep us in bondage and away from getting help. How do we get past these stumbling blocks if we can't seem to engage our will to choose to act for our good?

**5. What do the statements from Romans 8 mean for you?**

# God Can Heal Our Will

If we desire God's rest we must be able to activate our will. This is not mustering up our emotional energy to do God's will. (Warning: if you try to do this you are about to put yourself under the Law.) Most Christians know their spirits need saving and their minds need renewal. In today's culture we are also aware our emotions need healing. What if our heart says, "Yes I want to be all you have intended for me Lord," yet you are still stuck and can't activate your will? Have you considered your will might also need to be rescued by God?

God is willing to start at your deepest place of mistrust. If we know our will is in bondage and is not free to make healthy choices and decisions, what are we to do? Jesus told us all we need for God to work on our behalf is faith the size of a mustard seed. Remember our Strength in Weakness principle. God loves to work with small, tottering faith and show Himself strong on our behalf. Just your desire to be a part of God's will gives God enough to work with. I have discovered only one process for dealing with our wills, sins, shortcomings, wounds, disobedience, and lack of trust.

**6. In what areas of your life does God need to heal your will?**

## A Heart Attitude

The practical process for entering God's rest will always be the same as we resolve and God heals any issue confronting us. This process centers on a *heart attitude* regarding God and our particular issue. The words are not magical; the *heart attitude* is key.

We acknowledge to ourselves and to God we cannot continue this way one day longer. Our heart of heart cries out to God for intervention. Pride is banished as we become authentic and say, "Lord, I would rather have Your blessings than live one day longer with myself as I am. I am in bondage to (_____) and I cannot fix it. My faith is so tiny I have to rely on your faithfulness to me to change me. With the man Jesus asked, 'Do you want to be healed?' I too cry out, 'Lord, help my unbelief.' My will is in bondage, but I choose to trust You to set it free so I can choose Your will. I am the one trying to control my life. Forgive me. I throw my bondage onto You to fix."

I have modified four steps from the twelve steps of AA to use as a godly tool when we find ourselves in a tail spin. Remember your *heart attitude*, wanting to do God's will, is central to getting out of being stuck where you are.

### *Practical Steps to Doing God's Will:*

*Step 1*: **I admit I am powerless over (*insert your issue*), that my will, life, feelings, thoughts and or actions (*determine what they are*) – that my life has become unmanageable.**

"For I have the desire to do what is good, but I cannot carry it out." (Romans 7:18 b) In Step 1, I own my weakness. I come out of denial and suppression. I am ready for God's help. Pride is set aside. I acknowledge I cannot fix my situation.

*Step 2*: **I came to believe that a power greater than myself, Jesus Christ, can restore me to sanity.**

"…my grace is sufficient for you, for my power is made perfect in weakness." (2 Corinthians 12:9) In Step 2, I recognize that Jesus Christ's power is my only hope of change.

*Step 3*: **I am making a decision to turn my will, my life, and this issue over to the care of God.**

"For it is God Who works in you to will and to act according to His good purpose." (Philippians 2:13) In Step 3, I activate my will by giving my issue to God. I do this without judging myself. I remember I am a child coming to my wise, loving Father, seeking His help.

*Step 4*: **I will make a searching and fearless moral inventory of myself.**

"But let every person carefully scrutinize and examine and test his own conduct and his own work." (Galatians 6:4a, Amplified Bible) In Step 4, I begin my inner journey with the Lord and/or a counselor, to discover what my emotions and actions (on the outside) reveal about how God wants me to grow (on the inside).

Don't think there is any magic in saying these words. God heals in a sincere, honest heart attitude of the one praying. Deep within, we know we desperately need God. Words are nothing to God unless they are an expression of a heart attitude. Jesus told the Pharisees and scribes, "You are nullifying and making void and of no effect [the authority of] the word of God through your tradition." (Mark 7:13) Jesus was saying to them, *your heart is not in this.* God is saying, "You think you are doing My will when you pray by rote over and over again and by all your traditions, but you are not. Traditions are external behaviors. I want your heart. Bring your heart to Me in any condition it is in. My one requirement is to be real with Me and I will work on your behalf to heal you of your bondages."

In this heart attitude we pray, "God, You now have the issue. You are working all things together for my good, because I love You." (Romans 8:28) You will show me how and where I am taking control over my issue and not letting You keep it. Since You have my problem, I am going to rest emotionally and trust You, God, to do the work in me. My faith [trust] is weak but You are strong and trustworthy. Because You have given me everything I need for life and godliness, I will be using Your faith and not my own to trust You. I am determined not to pick up the problem again and if I do, it will be like a hot potato. I will drop it back into Your hands, Lord." You have entered God's Sabbath rest. Stay there as God works out your problem and gives you direction.

7. **As your heart is prepared, take the 4 steps toward entering God's rest. Journal your thoughts and feelings about this process.**

## The Apostle John's Story

The Apostle John called himself *the disciple Jesus loved* in the gospel book God inspired him to write about Jesus' life. John seemed to receive God's best and God's rest. This gospel is considered by most biblical scholars to be the most profound of the four gospels. New Christians are often directed to read the book of John as their first experience with reading the Bible. In the letter of 1 John, he eloquently wrote of love, as he personally knew and experienced a life transforming love. Consider John's story:

- John was one of three apostles closest to Jesus in His ministry.
- He saw Jesus transfigured, talking with Moses and Elijah on the Mount of Transfiguration.
- We find John resting his head on Jesus' chest during the Last Supper.
- From His cross, Jesus committed His own mother into John's care.
- John was the first disciple to reach Jesus' empty tomb, although as he hesitated outside, Peter went in first.
- Because of something Jesus said, other disciples questioned if John would live forever and not die. John straightened this out in his gospel.
- John saw and recorded what he saw in the book of Revelation, an amazing vision of the end of the world.
- Of the twelve apostles, he is the only one reported not to have died a martyr's death.

I remember once asking, "God, did You love John more than the other disciples?" This could not be true. I was confused. I believe the Lord said to me, "I love all of My disciples the same, just as I love all My children the same.

What is different about John is he, of all the apostles, was able to personally receive more from Me than the others, showing he genuinely trusted Me. As a result, John became an open vessel for Me to use."

Do you see the pivotal factor here? John was willing to receive, to accept as fact, and own for himself all that Jesus had for him. As a child trusts his father, John trusted God. John obviously *let go and let God* have his life. John lived out of the Sabbath rest of God.

**8. What do you learn from John's example of entering God's rest and trusting Him?**

## God's Rest Beckons Us Today

As Hebrews 4:1-11 informs us, we too are to "enter into the Sabbath rest as did God when He rested on the seventh day after He ceased from His own good works." I visualize putting my umbilical cord onto God, if you will, so that I am eternally connected to His love, His power, His acceptance and His identity. Through this cord I can experience the life of Christ flowing into me and receive all the nourishment I will ever need for growth, maturity, direction, and wisdom. This umbilical cord is similar to the branch Jesus spoke of in John 15:5-11:

*I am the vine, you are the branches; he who abides in Me and I in him, he bears much fruit, for apart from Me you can do nothing. If anyone does not abide in Me, he is thrown away as a branch and dries up; and they gather them, and cast them into the fire and they are burned. If you abide in Me, and My words abide in you, ask whatever you wish, and it will be done for you. My Father is glorified by this, that you bear much fruit, and so prove to be My disciples. Just as the Father has loved Me, I have also loved you; abide in My love. If you keep My commandments, you will abide in My love; just as I have kept My Father's commandments and abide in His love. These things I have spoken to you so that My joy may be in you, and that your joy may be made full.*

The vine sends nutrients to the branch and the branch accepts the vine's gift. The branch grows due to no effort on the branch's part. The same is true for the fruit. Suddenly, there is a tiny bud; the beginning fruit. The bud grows, yet the branch has done nothing except to receive the nutrients. Suddenly, from seemingly out of nowhere, a luscious fruit has grown to nourish others. Did the fruit come from the branch? No. It came from the vine. In the same way Jesus asks us to abide in Him. The part we play is to willingly abide and receive in Christ. He will produce the fruit in our lives first and then that fruit can be given away to others.

**9. How do you abide in the vine as Jesus tells us to do?**

# In Summary

God continues day and night, moment by moment, to call us into His rest. We can come to the place in our walk with the Lord where we can enter into God's Sabbath rest. Ending the war with ourselves and accepting ourselves with God Esteem, as God does, is one large step in that direction. Believing who you are in Christ and staying out from under the Law is another. Accepting God's strength for your inadequacies and setting boundaries will invite the peace of God.

Staying in His rest expands our understanding and experience of more and more of the heart of God. As God sets free the imprisoned areas of our lives, we will spend more and more time resting in His Sabbath rest. We are there when we can accept ourselves as imperfect children who are so loved by God that there is nothing we can't bring to Him. We can bring all areas of inadequacy in our lives to our Abba: be it our frustrations with our children, our marriages, our careers, our health, ourselves. God desires that this Sabbath rest be a way of life. It comes from trusting God to work out those things that we are powerless to change.

**Will you trust Him with all of your life, and find your Sabbath rest in Him?**

# SUPPLEMENTAL HELPS

## *Moving Towards Authenticity*

Hopefully these helps will facilitate your awareness of the principles covered in this book. I pray they will move you closer to God's Sabbath rest. As you partner with God more and more yokes of slavery will disappear. You will then experience more and more of God's peace for longer lengths of time.

## Beginning the Process:

### *Understanding Your Own Internal Dynamics*

God commands self-care. When Jesus says to love God, self, and neighbor with our heart, soul, mind, and strength, He refers to the four key areas that make us human: the spiritual, the emotional, the intellectual, and the physical. Most Christians understand taking care of the physical, even the intellectual, but the emotional part of ourselves? They go blank and have little understanding about how to go about taking care of their emotions.

Think of your emotions as God's information system. They inform us about our needs, our deepest beliefs, and longings. God operates in all of the same emotions we do. If that seems curious, reflect on Jesus. He cried. He got angry. He was depressed and experienced anxiety. He experienced abandonment from His Father and the people He came to give His life for. If you want to know God's emotions, look at Jesus.

All of our emotions are God-given; however, our emotions may be skewed to the point they are greatly out of proportion for the situation at hand. When an emotion is habitually too strong, the emotion is in control of us. On the other hand, our emotions may be so skewed in the opposite direction we feel little to nothing. Our emotions seem to be frozen and stifled to the point we not only do not feel strong negative emotions but also do not feel joyful emotions. Regardless of which end of the continuum you find yourself, our emotions can control us.

As Christians we have the fruit of the Spirit. Galatians 5:22 states, "But the fruit of the Spirit is love, joy, peace, longsuffering, kindness, goodness, faithfulness, meekness, self-control; against such there is no law." If we do not experience self-control then our emotions are far out of line with how God would want us to experience and express these emotions.

In *Helps #1* you will find a step-by-step process to help you unravel what is happening to you when you know your emotions are internally or externally out of control. Use the information to help you any time you experience your emotions taking a nosedive.

As you work through this process, use paper and pen to express your personal answers to any of the questions you feel pertinent to you and your situation. As you go through this, you will be amazed at what actually goes through our minds and our emotions in a split second. I was amazed as I wrote using this process.

The process seems long and it happens so fast, most of us don't even recognize what just happened to us. You may not know some of the answers to the questions. This indicates you are not as aware of your inner life as you could be. But don't despair, God wants to take you on an inner journey in order to heal and complete you in Christ. He will be your teacher. It would be a blessing if church members could help one another go through this process helping each other discover what exactly is happening in their minds and hearts.

## HELPS #1

# God, Why Has My Countenance Changed?

Use the sentence stems found under the heading *Put It All Together* as you go through the following process.

### *Pray*

Ask the Lord and the Holy Spirit to enter into this process with you, helping to make you aware of what is happening. What is sin? What are the wounds?

### *Commit to Healing*

A willful commitment to healing is necessary. Use your emotions as a signal to check in with yourself to find out what is going on. You can pray for God to remove a particular over-the-top emotion or behavior. It seems that until we have an awareness of what is going on inside of us and why, God generally will not heal something of which you are unaware. You need the same information God already has.

### Begin Awareness

Just a moment ago you were joyful and peaceful, and now you have taken a nosedive into some disquieting emotion. What just happened? You must first be aware when your countenance changes, then be committed being authentic, and transparent with yourself and with God. Don't write anything yet.

### Listen to Your Emotions

If you are not sure what to do with your emotions, a good place to start is to simply say to yourself, "I am feeling something. I wonder what it is." Do not name it yet.

Since emotions have a physiological expression, write all that apply on a piece of paper. Try to find where in your body you are feeling discomfort. Do a total body scan, starting from the top of your head, and think carefully about what you are feeling and where. Do you feel tension anywhere? Any butterflies? What is your body trying to tell you? If your chest feels tight, if your stomach is in knots, what could this mean? Write out all that apply.

### Identify and Name Your Emotions

Using *Helps #2*, Emotions, try to identify the word that denotes what you are experiencing. Is the identified emotion strong or moderate? Suppose your stomach is in knots. Maybe you feel as though an elephant sat on your chest. What emotion might this be? Are you experiencing anxiety? Do you feel guilt, anger, or sadness? The stronger and more chronic the emotion is, the more likely it is connected to your younger years and has been triggered in the present. Sometimes you are feeling numerous emotions at once. Begin using *Put it all Together*: I feel (_____)

### *Identify Your Trigger*

Ask yourself: "Why am I feeling this way right now?" Did someone say something to you that is just now registering with your emotions? Was it something your husband, child, or boss said? Did you say something to yourself or think something that triggered all of this? Was it something a friend said in a telephone conversation? Was it something you heard on the television? Was it your mother? Have you put yourself under the Law rather than grace? Have you judged or condemned yourself? Write your answer out based on what is happening to you right now.

### *Identify What You Told Yourself About Feeling these Emotions*

Once you identify the emotion(s) and the trigger, then identify what you are thinking about the particular emotion(s), such as: *I can't stand them. I will never make it. This is too much pain for one to bear*, etc.

### *Identify What You Told Yourself For Feeling These Emotions*

What do you think about yourself being anxious, angry, depressed? Are you angry with yourself for feeling these emotions? Are you disappointed with yourself? Are you telling yourself you are a failure? Are you telling yourself you should be stronger than this? Write your answer out.

### *Identify What You Told Yourself About the Person or Situation*

Example: *I hate my mother!! Working here is intolerable!*

### What Action Did You Take When the Emotions Flooded In?

Example: *I screamed at my mother and hung up the phone. I withdrew from everyone.* Write your action or non-actions out.

### Did You Self-Soothe? How?

This is how you try to pull all the pieces of yourself back together after the event. *You call a friend and go over the conversation with your mother with a friend. You go to the refrigerator and eat. You drink a glass of alcohol. You go out to a movie. You go to bed. You rationalize the situation. You can't self-soothe. You stay stuck in the pain and cannot get out of it. You read your Bible. You pray and nothing changes,* etc. Write out how you self-soothe.

### Can You Find a Time in Your Childhood That the Intensity of Your Emotions Matches the Present Emotions?

Journal what happened then.

## Put It All Together

Write out what has just happened in your life and what you are telling yourself about the event and what you are telling yourself about yourself. Use these sentence stems and a blank piece of paper or journal to help you process what is going on inside of you for the purpose of laying it at the Lord's feet.

*I felt* _____

*I was triggered when* _____

*This is what I told myself about my feelings. I said*
_____

*This is what I told myself about myself. I am* _____
*This is what I told myself about the other person or situation. I thought or said* _____

*As a result of my pain my action(s) were*_____
*I self-soothed by* _____
*This is what I am reminded of from my past* _____

## Example:

*I feel angry.* (What I feel.)
*When my mother tries to tell me what to do.* (The trigger: why I feel angry.)
*I am not supposed to feel anger toward my mother.* (What I told myself about my feelings.)
*I am such a wimp for letting her get to me like that.* (What I told myself about myself.)
*I screamed at her and slammed down the phone.* (What I did or did not do)
*I ate ice cream. I owe it to myself!* (How I self-soothed.)

### *Assess the Truth (Reality) of Your Evaluation of the Event*

Taking care of yourself means not only taking note of your troubled emotions and thoughts, but also asking: Am I telling myself the truth about this event? Could I be terrorizing, judging, interpreting this wrongly, condemning, berating, beating up on myself, pushing or quilting myself? Am I blaming another person for my own feelings and reactions?

Did I begin to list in my mind all the things the other person is thinking when he or she did or said what they did? Without knowing what they really meant by what they said, did I put a spin on what I think they meant? Remember, spins are not reality. They are just theories about what the other person's motive might have been. If I want to know reality, I will have to ask the other person what they meant by what they said, or did or dismiss my summation.

Also remember, it is not wrong to feel these feelings, but it is most unfortunate to live in a "fantasy of fear", anger, anxiety, or depression of something you have conjured up that may not even exist. This is why it is important to know what is happening in the inner part of your heart. Truth and reality are healing.

It is critical to connect how you feel to periods of time in your youth when you possibly felt the same way you do today. What in your past caused you pain? This pain from the past coupled with the events of today will put you over the top in your emotions. We all should feel emotions when things happen in our lives. God and Jesus have emotions as we who are made in His image also have emotions. It is the intensity of the emotions that wreck havoc in our lives.

Example: I was triggered when mother said, "Your friend Jenny really knows how to dress." I believe mother was telling me, "I wish you would get your act together and buy some mature clothes like Jenny." Is this really what your mother meant? Once I calm down, I will call and check this out with her.

Later: "Hi Mom, I am sorry I slammed down the phone. I took some time to think about what set me off. Here is what I want to ask you. When you mentioned Jenny and her ability to dress were you telling me I should dress better?"

What do you do with the answer? If Mom responds with, "No that was not my intent. I had not seen Jenny since your college days. When I bumped into her I thought, Wow! Has she grown up and look how lovely she dresses!" you will have to go with what her response is. Don't spin it again and say to yourself, "She is lying." She may be, but at least she heard what you had to say.

If your mother says, "Yes darling, I truly wish you would dress better" then make a request but do it with respect for her and respect for yourself. "Mother, if you are thinking about something you want from me, I am requesting you be direct with me and tell me straight up. Just come out with it, please. I have been receiving covert messages from you since elementary school. This way I don't have to guess what you mean. When you do bring up things that don't please you, I will take your advice under consideration. However, since I am an adult now, I may or may not act on your advice."

Continue to be a broken record with your mother until she gets your point and backs off. These few sentences are far better than sleepless nights of anger or many gallons of ice cream. If your behavior is never addressed, your mother's behavior will go on until she dies—and so might your anger, unless it is dealt with.

### Cast Your Cares Upon Jesus

God wants to heal your heart. He wants you to know what needs to be healed, then for you to own what needs healing, and come into agreement with Him. As you have greater awareness of your feelings and thoughts and subsequent actions or no actions with yourself or another, cast that dynamic (care) over onto Jesus. Confess your part in the skirmish. Then acknowledge that you and God are now on the same page. In humility ask God to calm down the over-the-top emotion, because you know you do not have the power to overcome it. Have an attitude of "I need help."

Remember, it is all right to need help. Helping is one of God's greatest capacities. He is committed to help you become more and more Christ-like in your relationships with Him, yourself, and others. Tell Him you trust Him to heal you, but only if you really do. If not, start just with your needing help. Once your problem is in His hands, you do not have to try to fix yourself, other than putting yourself in a healing environment which could be a safe counseling group, a Bible study that is safe and authentic, or with a Christian counselor. Rest in God's Sabbath rest as you wait to experience more and more sanctification of your heart by God.

**An Example of How to Pray**

*Lord, I am holding resentment in my heart toward my mother. She tells me things I should and should not do, like I am still a child. I also judge her and conjure up in my mind what I think she meant in our conversation. I realize this too is a sin. Lord, I want to face her and address this issue with her, because things are just getting worse between us. I am afraid. I need Your strength and healing hand in this. I throw my sins and myself onto You and ask forgiveness. I admit I cannot fix myself or my mother. My only hope is in Your fixing me and healing me so I can deal with my mother in a respectful way. I am going to rest in Your power to do this thing in and through me. In Jesus' name. Amen.*

**HELPS #2**

# Feeling Word List

This is a list of negative feelings to help you determine what you really are experiencing in the moment. You may list several feelings for one event. This helps you with self-awareness. Self-awareness is important for authenticity.

**Mild:** unpopular, listless, moody, lethargic, gloomy, dismal, discontented, tired, indifferent, unsure, impatient, dependent, unimportant, regretful, bashful, puzzled, self-conscious, edgy, upset, reluctant, timid, mixed-up, sullen, provoked.

**Moderate:** suspicious, envious, enmity, aversion, dejected, unhappy, bored, forlorn, disappointed, wearied, inadequate, ineffectual, helpless, resigned, apathetic, shy, uncomfortable, baffled, confused, nervous, tempted, tense, worried, perplexed, troubled, disdainful, contemptuous, alarmed, annoyed, provoked.

**Strong:** disgusted, resentful, bitter, detested, fed up, frustrated, sad, depressed, sick, dissatisfied, fatigued, worn out, useless, weak, hopeless, forlorn, rejected, guilty, embarrassed, inhibited, bewildered, frightened, anxious, dismayed, apprehensive, disturbed, antagonistic, vengeful, indignant, mad, torn.

**Intense:** hate, unloved, abhor, despised, angry, hurt, miserable, pain, lonely, cynical, worthless, impotent, futile, accursed, abandoned, estranged, degraded, humiliated, shocked, panicky, trapped, horrified, afraid, scared, terrified, threatened, infuriated, furious, exhausted.

## HELPS #3

# Identity Verses

This is a partial listing of the verses I wrote out as I discovered my identity in Christ. The confession comes first, and then the verse. It will help you to say these out loud. I pray they will help you know how much you are loved.

### *I am born again!*

"Blessed be the God and Father of our Lord Jesus Christ, who according to His great mercy has caused us to be born again to a living hope through the resurrection of Jesus Christ from the dead." (1 Peter 1:3)

### *I am a new creation, in Christ!*

"Therefore if any man is in Christ, he is a new creature; the old things passed away; behold new things have come." (2 Corinthians 5:17)

### *I am righteous, in Christ!*

"He made Him who knew no sin to become sin on our behalf that we might become the righteousness of God in Him." (2 Corinthians 5:21)

### *There is no more condemnation for me because I am in Christ!*

"There is therefore now no condemnation for those who are in Christ Jesus." (Romans 8:1)

### *All my sins are forgiven, in Christ!*

"In Him we have redemption through His blood, the forgiveness of our trespasses, according to the riches of His grace." (Ephesians 1:7)

### *I am a saint!*

"To the church of God which is at Corinth, to those who have been sanctified in Christ Jesus, saints by calling, with all who in every place call upon the name of our Lord Jesus Christ, their Lord and ours." (1 Corinthians 1:2)

### *I know I have eternal life!*

"These things I have written to you who believe in the name of the Son of God, in order that you may know that you have eternal life." (1 John 5:13)

### *I am a citizen of heaven!*

"For our citizenship is in heaven, from which also we eagerly wait for a Savior, the Lord Jesus Christ." (Philippians 3:20)

### *I have been chosen by God and I am holy and blameless!*

"Just as He chose us in Christ before the foundation of the world, that we should be holy and blameless before God in love." (Ephesians 1:4)

### *Christ lives in me! Jesus is my hope of glory.*

"This is the mystery which has been hidden from the past ages and generations; but has now been manifested to His saints, to whom God willed to make known what is the riches of the glory of this mystery among the Gentiles, which is—Christ in you, the hope of glory." (Colossians 1:26-27)

### *I have been placed into Christ! I am a son/daughter of God!*

"For all of you are all sons of God through faith in Christ Jesus. For all of you who were baptized into Christ have clothed yourselves with Christ." (Galatians 3:26-27)

### *I have been sealed in Christ with the Holy Spirit!*

"In Him, you also, after listening to the message of truth, the gospel of your salvation having also believed, you were sealed in Him with the Holy Spirit of promise." (Ephesians 1:13)

### *I am indwelt by the Holy Spirit! I am the temple of God.*

"Do you not know that you are a temple of God, and that the Spirit of God dwells in you?" (1 Corinthians 3:16)

### *I am dead to sin! I am alive to God!*

"Consider yourself to be dead to sin, but alive to God in Christ Jesus." (Romans 6:11)

### *I have the mind of Christ!*

"We have the mind of Christ." (1 Corinthians 2:16b)

### *I am welcomed in God's throne room!*

"Let us therefore draw near with confidence to the throne of grace, that we may receive mercy and may find grace to help in time of need." (Hebrews 4:16)

### *God loves me. I am seated in the heavenlies with Christ!*

"But God, being rich in mercy, because of His great love with which He loved us, even when we were dead in our transgressions, made us alive together with Christ (by grace you have been saved) and raised us up with Jesus, and seated us with Him in the heavenly places, in Christ Jesus." (Ephesians 2:4-6)

***I cannot be separated from the love of God regardless of my failures!***

"I am convinced that neither death, nor life, nor angels, nor principalities, nor things present, nor things to come, nor powers, nor height, nor depth, nor any other created thing, shall be able to separate us from the love of God, which is in Christ Jesus our Lord." (Romans 8:38-39)

***I know the truth and I am free.***

"You shall know the truth and the truth shall set you free." (John 8:32)

***I have met the truth and He has set me free.***

"Jesus said to him, 'I am the way the truth, and the life; no one comes to the Father but through me.'" (John 14:6)

***I cannot work for my salvation; it is a free gift from God to me!***

"For by grace you have been saved through faith; and that not of yourselves, it is the gift of God; not as a result of works, that no one should boast." (Ephesians 2:8-9)

***I love God! I love me! I love you!***

"You shall love the Lord your God with all you heart, and with all your soul, and with all your mind. And the second is like it. You shall love your neighbor as you do yourself. On these two commandments depend the whole Law and the Prophets." (Matthew 22:37-40)

*I can do whatever God asks me to do!*

"I can do all things through Christ who strengthens me." (Philippians 4:13)

**HELPS #4**

# Testing/Trials/Suffering Paradigm

How many times have you heard a Christian who is in the midst of some considerable difficulty say, "I know God is trying to teach me something in all of this, but I don't know what it is." Or, "Why is this happening to me?"

These questions are valid, but I have rarely known a Christian who could sufficiently answer either of the questions. As a result, the Christian agonizes in emotional and spiritual turmoil.

Testing, whether you believe it is orchestrated by God or that God allows man's free will to play itself out: your reaction to testing gives you the opportunity to be aware of where God wants to work in your life. It is a *heads up* from God. The quicker you let God get started working on you the quicker peace will come.

You may have played no part in the difficulty you are experiencing; however, if you will be truly honest with yourself about what you are thinking and feeling about the difficulty and admit it to yourself, you will be able to definitively know the answer to what God is trying to teach you and where God wants to work in your life.

Your pain reaction to testing has no condemnation in it from God. Your reaction is God's way of communicating with you what He wants to change in your life. *Something is wrong Lord. Help me know what you know.*

Testing allows those things of which God is aware and you are not to rise into your consciousness and emotions for the purpose of healing.

The Spirit of God cannot lead you to a place you are not even aware exists, unless:

- *You become aware.*
- *You and God are in agreement about that which is to be healed.*
- *You acknowledge your inability to change yourself.*
- *You continuously put your reactions, thoughts, and feelings into God's hand.*
- *You rest in God's capacity to heal you and make you more Christ-like over time.*

God in His love and mercy and perfect commitment to make you into the image of His Son will not allow negative attitudes, thought patterns, false beliefs, or unhealthy sinful actions to continue to control you, especially when unbeknown to you. Do not condemn yourself. Get into agreement with God and admit God's revelation to you is right on. Know that when you are weak that is when God can be strong on your behalf. Rejoice because God is getting ready to set you free! But we need to know from what He is freeing us.

## HELPS #5

# Meditative Prayer

Meditative prayer has a long history in Christianity. Put simply, meditative prayer is a state of being where you enter into the world of God as He has proclaimed it and rest in Him in His truth and reality.

- Find a quiet environment where you can be uninterrupted.
- Choose only *one* of the statements at a time found below to meditate on.
- Meditate on the meaning for you personally.
- Ruminate on the statement by saying it to yourself as often as you want.
- Take a passive, receiving attitude that enables you to receive from the God you know.
- Maintain a comfortable physical position, removing all pressure, strain, and demands on your body. Close your eyes if you choose.
- Think of God as sustainer, encourager, re-newer, healer, and friend.

## Statements

*I am not required to be perfect.*

*I go to Jesus as one who is heavy burdened and discouraged and He gives my soul relief and rest.*

*I take His yoke upon myself and learn of Jesus.*

*Jesus is gentle with me.*

*I find refreshment, recreation, and blessed quiet for my soul in Jesus.*

*Jesus' yoke is not harsh, sharp, or pressing.*

*Jesus is gracious, pleasant, and compassionate with me.*

*As Jesus bears my burden with me, my burden becomes lighter.*

*I am accepted in the beloved, just as I am.*

*I, like John the apostle, put my head on Jesus' breast and rest in His acceptance of me.*

## HELPS #6

# Confession of Faith

The only qualification for being a child of God is summed up in Romans 10:9-10.

> *⁹If you acknowledge and confess with your lips that Jesus is Lord, and in your heart believe [adhere to, trust in, and rely on the truth] that God raised Him from the dead, you will be saved.*
>
> *¹⁰For with the heart a person believes [adheres to, trusts in, and relies on Christ] and so is justified [declared righteous, acceptable to God], and with the mouth he confesses [declares openly and speaks out freely his faith]) and confirms his salvation.*

These two verses say an authentic Christian can acknowledge in the heart, not just the head, and speak out loud, that Jesus is Lord and that God raised Jesus from the dead. If these qualifications are met, you are saved, justified, declared righteous, and acceptable to God. We can openly speak out freely, "Jesus is Lord of my life."

If you are already a Christian, you can know by these two verses that you are saved. If you are not a Christian and you believe these two verses, then close your eyes and tell God you believe with your heart the best you can that Jesus is Lord and that God did raise Jesus from the dead. Thank Him for saving you, justifying you, declaring you righteous, and making you acceptable to God, in Jesus' name. Now go and tell someone with your mouth that Jesus is your Lord.

The Good News of Jesus Christ is so simple we can miss it altogether. Either God is telling the truth and you are now saved, or He is lying and you are not saved. God does not lie. You were born once into your family of origin. Now you have been born again, but this time into the family of God. Welcome!!

**HELPS #7**

# Grace

In times of trial and heartache, in times of failure and humanness, in times of sheer willful disobedience, in times of temptation and fall, where can we find someone to render us fit, to render us loved, to render us accepted? We find it in the God of grace.

### *Where does grace come from?*

"For the law was given through Moses; grace and truth were realized through Jesus Christ." (John 1:17)

### *How does one get salvation?*

"For by grace you have been saved through faith and that not of yourselves, it is the gift of God, not as a result of works, that no one should boast." (Ephesians 2:8-9)

### *To whom is grace given?*

"For all have sinned and fall short of the glory of God, being justified is a gift of God by grace through redemption which is in Christ Jesus." (Romans 3:23-24)

### *What is your standing as a believer in Christ Jesus?*

"You have been introduced by faith into this grace in which we stand." (Romans 5:1-2)

*Where can grace be found?*

"Where sin abounds, grace does much more abound." (Romans 5:20)

*What are you beholding to, grace or the law?*

"You are not under the law but under grace." (Romans 6:14-15)

*Can you do anything to either lose God's grace or to get God's grace?*

If salvation is by grace [a free gift], then salvation is no longer on the basis of works; otherwise grace is no longer grace. (see Romans 11:6)

## HELPS #8

# Poems and Prose

*I Am a Friend to Myself*

> *\*Dear Lord*
> *Today I am on my own side. I choose to*
> *Befriend myself and be on my own team,*
> *Which means I will not focus my energies*
> *Today on judging, criticizing, or demeaning*
> *Myself in any way. It is my responsibility*
> *To teach others how to treat me by the way I*
> *Treat myself.*
> *When I put these words into action, it*
> *Means that I don't have to constantly point*
> *Out my faults to myself and to others*
> *Around me. When I am for me, it means I*

*Will not create my own anxiety by giving*
*Myself negative messages. I will not be an*
*Enemy to myself.*
*\*Today I affirm, "God and I will*
*Always be with me and for me."*
*In Jesus' name, Amen.*

Daily Affirmations by Rokelle Learner
(\*Added by this author)

## Quotes

"Punitive false guilt feelings are a self-centered form of punishment designed to atone for one's failures. Feelings of punitive guilt are based on anger and self-rejection. Punitive false guilt is focused more on past failures. Constructive guilt (conviction) is oriented toward future changes." *(Cecil Osborn)*

"Lord, help me let go of how I think my life should be, so I can live the life You created for me." *(Unknown)*

"The truth of the matter is that we all come to God with a tangled mass of motives: altruistic and selfish, merciful and hateful, loving and bitter. Frankly, on this side of eternity we will never unravel the good from the bad, the pure from the impure. But what I have come to see is that God is big enough to receive us with all our mixture. We do not have to be bright, or pure, or filled with faith, or anything. That is what grace means; not only are we saved by grace, we live by it as well." *(Richard Foster)*

"If you are not honest with yourself; how can you be honest with God? And if you cannot be honest with God, how can He help you?" *(Cecil Osborn)*

# God's Love Letter to You

Dearly Beloved,

I am the Lord, the compassionate and gracious God, slow to anger, abounding in love and faithfulness, maintaining love to thousands. Greater love has no one than this, than to lay down one's life for his friends. I demonstrated My own love for you in this: while you were still a sinner, I died for you. For great is My love, reaching to the heavens; My faithfulness reaches to the skies! I have loved you with an everlasting love; I have drawn you with loving-kindness. I am faithful to all My promises and loving toward all I have made. I uphold all those who fall and lift up all who are bowed down. I am near to all who call on Me, to all who call on Me in truth. I fulfill the desires of those who fear Me. I hear their cry and save them. I am love.

Delight yourself in Me and I will give you the desires of your heart. I know the plans I have for you, plans to prosper you and not to harm you, plans to give you a future and a hope. Trust in Me with all your heart and don't lean on your own understanding; in all your ways acknowledge Me, and I will direct your paths. I will instruct you and teach you in the ways you should go; I will counsel you and watch over you. I Myself will go before you and will be with you; I will never leave you nor forsake you. Do not be afraid; do not be discouraged. I am with you; I am Your helper. Though the mountains be shaken and the hills be removed, yet My unfailing love for you will not be shaken.

Cast your cares on Me and I will sustain you; I will never let the righteous fall. If you listen to Me, you will live in safety and be at ease, without fear or harm. I will watch over your life. I am close to the brokenhearted and save those who are crushed in spirit. A righteous man may have many troubles, but I will deliver him from them all! So do not fear, for I am with you. I will uphold you with My righteous right hand. Come to Me all who are weary and burdened and I will give you rest. Learn from Me for I am gentle and humble in heart, and you will find rest for your souls. Cast all your anxiety on Me because I care for you.

Because you love Me, I will rescue you. I will protect you, for you acknowledge My name. You will call upon Me and I will answer you. I will be with you in trouble. I will deliver you and honor you. Since I Am for you, who can be against you? Who shall separate you from My love? Neither death nor life, nor angels nor demons, neither the present nor the future, nor any powers, neither height nor depth, nor anything else in all creation will be able to separate you from My love. My love endures forever!

With all my love,
*GOD*

(Paraphrased from: Ex. 34: 6-7; John 15:13; Rom. 5:8; Ps. 57:10; Jer. 31:3; Ps. 145:13-14, 18-19; 1 John 4:8; Ps. 37:4; Jer. 29:11; Prov. 3:5-6; Ps. 32:8; Deut. 31:8; Ps. 118:7; Is. 54:10; Ps. 55:22; Prov. 1:33; Ps. 121:7; Ps. 34:18-19; Is. 41:10; Matt. 11:28-29; 1 Peter 5:7; Ps. 91:14-15; Rom. 8:31, 38; Ps. 118:1)

**HELPS #9**

# An Insight of Mine

As Paul said on a few occasions, "*this may be of me and not of the Lord.*" The insight I have regarding Jesus' hard sayings may also be from me and not of the Lord. This insight is meant to help you better understand where Jesus was coming from when He told us numerous tough things God wants our lives to be. I pray it helps take the judgment off you.

***My Insight***: Clients often quote something Jesus said in the gospels as a way of contradicting something I have said about God's grace and mercy. I may have said something like, "God accepts us the way were are; sins, dysfunctions and all." They might come back with, "But Jesus said we are to be perfect as His Father is perfect." Matthew 5:38

I then ask them, "When did the New Covenant (New Testament) actually begin?" Most say at the birth of Jesus. Often, they rightly say, in the heart of God before the foundation of the world. Then I say, "But when in time and space did the New Testament (Covenant) come into fruition? What point in time was there the switch from the law to grace?"

They think and then say, "When Jesus rose from the dead and ascended into heaven." I go with this. Some theologian may tell me it was when Jesus went to heaven and put His blood on the mercy seat for each and every one of us and then came back to earth for forty days and nights.

Regardless, the point I am trying to make is: when Jesus walked this earth for three-and-a-half years He did so under the Old Covenant. Matthew, Mark, Luke and John are about Jesus' work here on earth prior to His taking our sins on himself and initiating a new Covenant.

He lived out the Old Covenant (the Law) for us. Why? Because He knew as His Father knew, neither the children of Israel nor we ourselves could ever live up to the teachings of the Law. Thus during his time on earth when Jesus spoke, He spoke of the perfect will of the Father that you and I cannot attain.

Some of Jesus' hard sayings are better understood knowing what I believe Jesus was trying to get across to the people. When He made statements such as, Matthew 5:28 "But I say to you that everyone who so much as looks at a woman with evil desire for her has already committed adultery with her in his heart;" I believe He was trying to make it very clear, "It is impossible to measure up to my Father's

Law." Even if you look good on the outside God knows your true motivations. You can never "be perfect as my Father is perfect."

It seems Jesus was trying to reach those who truly wanted a relationship with God and would drop their pride and cry out, "Lord I can't do that. I need help. I am without hope. I need a savior to do for me what I can not do for myself; live a perfect sinless life for me, be punished in my place and then give me, the sinner: forgiveness."

***In Summary:***There is a tension we must accept and learn to appreciate in order to be at peace. Our hearts desire is to please God and to allow His Spirit to transform us out of our sins little by little, but at the same time know we will never measure up to all of God's commands. We will fail. We are not to condemn ourselves. We are to appreciate what Jesus has done for us and take our own judgment off of ourselves and live at peace in the Family of God.

**HELPS #10**

# Principles for Healthy Relationships

- Blaming others instead of looking at ourselves will bring more pain into our lives and the other's life.
- Our Christian maturation is about our growing, not the other person changing.
- God does care about our external circumstances but if He sees something in our hearts that needs to be changed, then *the Inside Out principle* becomes operational.
- It is possible to live life to its fullest, even if the circumstances do not change.
- We need to ask God to help us find the sin, the wounds of our past, or the lie that needs to be healed.

- God wants us to focus on our reactions to the other person, rather than focus blame on the other person.
- The way we know what God wants to heal in us is to take stock of any emotional dissonance, any harmful thoughts or actions that arise over and over again within ourselves.
- Emotional pain is like God's finger pointing to what needs to be changed by Him.
- I cannot fix another person. I have only been given authority to allow God to fix me.
- When we try to fix our external circumstance involving other people, we block God and His work of grace in our lives and their lives.

## HELPS #11

### *How Negative Self-Talk Takes Hold*

- We lack knowledge regarding the significance of having a healthy relationship with ourselves.
- Our churches espouse any regard for oneself as a sin.
- We see scripture in only one context, not seeing the full counsel of God on the subject of loving yourself.
- Our sin nature perverts the love that God intends to be healthy and we aggrandize ourselves.
- Satan loves to fan the flames of our negative self-talk so we may very well reap our own self-fulfilling prophecy, such as, "I will never amount to anything." He loves to keep us from walking in agreement with who God says we are in Christ. We wrongly believe that poor-mouthing ourselves is godly humility.
- Negative self-talk is all we know. Many of us have been treated this way in our families of origin. We just continue the negative dialog in our heads.

- We fear being rejected or abandoned. We do not feel safe enough to be authentic, open, honest, and real. So, we stay hidden.
- We misinterpret what another person says or does. We give the action our own negative interpretation as to what we think the person meant, rather than asking the person what they meant. We believe our own theory and then live out of that non-reality. This spin is a negative cycle that wounds us and may wound the other person, as well.
- We falsely believe we are the only ones who feel this way.

## Helps #12

These 12 steps can be used for anything you feel is pulling you away from and adversely affecting you, your family relations, your work and your relationship with God. Instead of the word alcohol, put in your weakness such as: work, anger, gossip, golf, fear, gardening, loving my family more than God, chewing gum and on and on.

# 12 STEPS OF ALCOHOLICS ANONYMOUS

## With Biblical References

*1. We admitted we were powerless over alcohol... that our lives had become unmanageable.*

"I know that nothing good lives in me, that is, in my sinful nature. For I have the desire to do what is good, but I cannot carry it out." (Romans 7:18)

*2. We came to believe that a Power greater than ourselves could restore us to sanity.*

"...my grace is sufficient for you, for my POWER is made perfect in weakness." (2 Corinthians 12:9)
"...for it God Who works in you to will and act according to His good purpose..." (Phil. 2:13)

*3. We made a decision to turn our will and our lives over to the care of GOD as we understood Him.*

"... If anyone would come after me, he must deny himself and take up his cross daily and follow me." (Luke 9:23**)

**4. We made a searching and fearless moral inventory of ourselves.**

"Let us examine our ways and test them, and let us return to the Lord." (Lamentations 3:40)

**5. We admitted to GOD, to ourselves and to another human being the exact nature of our wrongs.**

"Therefore confess your sins to each other and pray for each other so that you may be healed." (James 5:16)

**6. We were entirely ready to have GOD remove all these defects of character.**

"If you are willing and obedient, you will eat the best from the land." (Isaiah 1:19)

**7. We humbly asked Him to remove all our shortcomings.**

"Humble yourselves before the Lord, and He will lift you up." (James 4:10)

**8. We made a list of all persons we had harmed and became willing to make amends to them all.**

"Therefore, if you are offering your gift at the altar and there remember that your brother has something against you, leave your gift there in front of the altar. First go and be reconciled to your brother; then come and offer your gift." (Matthew 5:23, 24**)

**9. We made direct amends to such people wherever possible, except when to do so would injure them or others.**

"Give and it shall be given you. A good measure, pressed down, shaken together and running over, will be poured into your lap. For with the measure you use, it will be measured to you." (Luke 6:38**)

**10. We continued to take personal inventory and when we were wrong, we promptly admitted it.**

"For by the grace given me I say to every one of you: Do not think of yourself more highly than you ought, but rather think of yourself with sober judgment, in accordance with the measure of faith GOD has given you." (Romans 12:3)

**11. We sought through prayer and meditation to improve our conscious contact with GOD as we understood Him, praying only for knowledge of His will, and the power to carry that out.**

"May the words of my mouth and the meditation of my heart be pleasing in your sight, O Lord, my Rock and my Redeemer." (Psalm 19:14)
"Let the word of Christ dwell in you richly..." (Col. 3:16)

**12. Having had a spiritual awakening as the result of these steps, we tried to carry this message to alcoholics, and practice these principles in all our affairs.**

"Brothers, if someone is caught in a sin, you who are spiritual should restore him gently. But watch yourself, or you also may be tempted. Carry each other's burdens, and in this way you will fulfill the law of Christ." (Galatians 6:1-2)

  ** *Indicates these are words of Christ*